# The
# Bumper Joke
# Book

# The Bumper Joke Book

by

Kevin Goldstein-Jackson

# Contents

# Dedication

This book is dedicated to my wife, Mei Leng, who makes my life so much better, and to my two daughters, Sing Yu and Kimberley, on whom all the jokes have been tested; and to all my friends, relatives and acquaintances around the world who have made helpful suggestions and provided some jokes.

It is also dedicated to the Elliot brothers and their late father who have, for many years, encouraged my joke book production and succeeded in spreading humour around the world.

# Introduction

This book contains 1,250 jokes. Many can be used to provide a chuckle amongst friends, produce a smile in difficult situations, some laughter in otherwise dull speeches, act as a pin to pop pomposity and as weapons of crass destruction. Some, intentionally, may produce groans ...

But have you ever wondered where jokes come from? And how you can create your own humour? Some are based on true events. For example, joke 1232 about a bus journey in Bournemouth actually happened to me.

When I was a small boy my English teacher read aloud extracts from books – but slipped in humour. For example, he would read 'she opened the door in her nightdress' – then pause briefly for effect – and add his own comment 'funny place to have a door'.

This excited my interest in the use of words and much humour can be derived from the different ways in which a word can be used, or the various ways of interpreting everyday sayings or expressions or even deconstructing a word to find humour.

For example, take the word 'contact', which has two syllables and thus inspired the joke: He's very much a contact man – all con and no tact.

Then there was the young man who said he had a sweater for Christmas – but he really wanted someone who sighed or screamed.

Similar sounding words can produce humour – some of it childish, such as: What do jumbos wear around their bottoms? Ele-pants.

Thinking back to childhood and parents' exhortations can also promote humour. My mother taught me all sorts of things – like contortionism ('look at all the dirt on the back of your neck') and osmosis ('shut your mouth and eat your dinner').

This leads to thinking about other possible wise sayings – such as: 'No one hears you until you fart.' 'For every action there is an equal and opposite government programme.' 'It is unwise to take sleeping pills and a laxative at the same time.' 'No matter how many times a married man changes his job he still has the same boss.'

Listen out for particular lines in conversations and think how to add something humorous – although sometimes it is wise to keep quiet. For example, at a hotel a porter asks someone 'Can I carry your bag?' One response might be 'No, she can walk.'

A boring speaker drones on and on and then says 'on the other hand ...' you could think/say 'you have different fingers'.

If someone says something is 'very character building' then what character are they building? Or their boringness reminds you that light travels faster than sound which is why the speaker appeared bright until he spoke.

Reading the newspapers can lead to absurd thoughts. Lots of people are 'killed in cold blood'. Where do they get all this blood to drown them in? 'The police posted a man at the door.' How did they get him through the letterbox? 'Police are canvassing the area.' By covering the area with tents?

Newspapers are full of surveys and statistics. 'Seventy-five per cent of married men cheat in the USA' – to which you might add 'the rest cheat in Europe'.

The business pages often have news of management changes which leads to the thought: 'Seagull managers' – they fly in, make a lot of noise, crap everywhere, and then quickly leave.

On TV, watch out for dialogue that can be misinterpreted. When a policeman approaches a building, takes out a gun and says to a colleague 'cover me' – imagine if his colleague threw a blanket over him.

'He was scared half to death.' What happens if he was scared twice?

'He had a name to be reckoned with.' Why? Was his name John Calculator?

Or watch the adverts. 'Guaranteed weed free lawn' – they don't charge anything for the weeds. For some products the makers claim 'nothing acts faster' – so why buy it if nothing is faster?

Jokes change over time. When someone comes up to me and says 'have you heard the latest joke about ...' (and they name a particular politician) I might say 'No' and they tell me the joke – but I may well have heard it before, but the subject then had been a particular nationality or a blonde woman or a foolish man and *not* a politician.

Political correctness has to be followed. A man cannot be a male chauvinist pig – he just has swine empathy. No one is 'balding' – they simply have follicle regression.

Just thinking of politics leads to remembering a good definition of a politician: someone who shakes your hand before an election and your confidence afterwards.

Look around you – humour is everywhere – and there's a lot of it in this book.

Happy joking!

KG-J

# AGE & AGEING

**1.** As I've grown older I've realised that money is not everything – but it certainly ensures that the children still visit.

**2.** By the time he had made enough money to be able to eat in the finest restaurants, drink the finest wines and cavort with the most beautiful women – his doctor restricted his diet, banned alcohol and told him not to exert himself too much.

**3.** I knew I was getting old when I turned to look at the little old lady I was helping across the road and realised she was my wife.

**4.** You know you're getting old when almost every story you tell begins, 'Back when I was your age' or 'When I was younger.'

**5.** As you get older you have to be kinder to your children. They are the ones who may eventually have to choose your nursing home.

**6.** He hasn't got an enemy in the whole world. He's so old he's outlived all the people he cheated, ruined and lied about.

**7.** The older she gets, the more attractive she looks . . . by the time she's 100 years old she might look quite reasonable.


**8.** James told his wife, 'I think I've aged remarkably well. Women still chase after me.'

His wife replied, 'That's because you still keep stealing their handbags and running away.'


**9.** When I asked my two-year-old nephew if he could tell me how old he was, he replied, 'I'm not old – I'm nearly new.'


**10.** He knew he was getting old when his wife said his actions creak louder than his words.


**11.** She was such an old blood-sucking creature they called her a granpire.


**12.** She's so old that the antique jewellery she wears she bought when it was new.


**13.** Instead of getting older and *wiser* my husband is getting older and *wider*.


**14.** My wife and I were born in the same year. But when I reached 40 I took a day off. On her birthday my wife took a year off.

**15.** My husband decided to bake me a cake for my birthday – but unfortunately when he put it in the oven the candles melted all over it.

**16.** She's so absent-minded she even forgot her twin sister's birthday.

**17.** I wouldn't say my wife tells lies about her age – but does she really expect people to believe that she gave birth to our son at the age of three?

**18.** You know you're old when you recall that in your youth a kiss happened at the end of a beautiful evening. Today a kiss means it's the start of a *fantastic* evening.

**19.** She knew she was getting old when she thought more about pensions than passions.

**20.** I think I've just reached the out-age. When you reach 60, everything seems to spread out, fall out or wear out!

**21.** She asked him if he thought her face was starting to show her age. He replied that it was difficult for him to tell, as there were so many wrinkles.

**22.** One thing I've noticed about old age is that it makes women's arms get shorter. For example, when I got married my wife could easily put her arms right around me – now she can't.

# ANIMALS & THE NATURAL WORLD

**23.** Tom was very annoyed with his parrot. Every time someone visited Tom's home, the parrot would say something offensive.

Tom tried to make the parrot behave. When the parrot shouted 'Fat cow, fat cow' at Tom's mother, Tom flicked cold water at his pet.

When the parrot shouted obscene four-letter words at a visiting priest, Tom hastily covered the parrot's cage and kept the bird in the dark for a whole day.

The final straw came when the parrot made such disgusting comments to Tom's girlfriend that she stormed out of the house. Tom scolded the bird, took it out of its cage, put it in a strong transparent plastic box with air holes, and put it in the freezer. He told the bird: 'It's time you cooled down.'

Ten minutes later, Tom opened the freezer, and the parrot said: 'Sorry! Sorry! I've learnt my lesson. I'll behave. But please let me know what the chicken in here said to annoy you ...'


**24.** 'How is your yearling coming along?' one gentleman asked another as they chatted in the Silver Ring at Ascot.

'It died,' said the other.

'That must have lost you a fortune, with the training fees and everything,' sympathized the other man.

'No, I made a profit actually,' the owner chuckled. 'I raffled him at £10 a ticket.'

'Didn't anyone sue you for fraud?'

'No. The winner got a bit shirty but I sent *him* his money back!'


**25.** Two men bought themselves a horse each and decided to keep them in the same field.

'How shall we tell which horse is which?' asked Paul.

'I'll tie a blue ribbon to the tail of my horse,' replied Peter.

Unfortunately, the ribbon on Paul's horse fell off one day in Paul's absence, so the two were again faced with the problem of deciding which horse was which.

'I know,' suggested Paul, 'you have the brown horse and I'll have the white one.'


**26.** He's devoted most of his life to giving money to sick animals. It's such a shame that the horses he bets on are so ill.


**27.** When my daughter asked me, 'Has anyone seen the cat bowl?' I said, 'Yes. He scored three strikes in a row at the bowling alley last night.'


**28.** The difference between dogs and cats is that dogs have owners, while cats have servants.


**29.** My daughter's very pleased – her cat won a milk-drinking contest by five laps.

**30.** The main difference between cats and dogs is that if you have a pet dog and call its name, it will come to you. If you have a pet cat and call its name, it will take the message that you are calling it and may come back to you.

**31.** What's got four legs and an arm?
An angry dog.

**32.** I know a man who called his dog Rolex because it was a watch dog.

**33.** When I visited my young nephew I noticed that his dog was scratching. 'Does your dog have fleas?' I asked.
My nephew looked at me scornfully and replied: 'Surely you know that dogs don't have fleas – they have puppies.'

**34.** A farmer friend of mine keeps telling jokes to chickens. He's hoping to turn them into comedi-hens. At least they might appreciate corny jokes ...

**35.** My young cousin lives on a farm and was given a pet duck for his birthday. He was soon proudly boasting that the duck could say its own name.
'What *is* the duck's name?' I asked.
My cousin replied: 'Its name is Quack.'

**36.** When I was on holiday I suddenly saw a large tiger. At first, we just stared at each other – then it slowly moved towards me. I stood still and silent.

As the tiger got nearer it growled and then roared as it leapt straight towards me. But I stood my ground and did not flinch.

Then I moved away and went to look at the lions in the next cage in the zoo.

**37.** The world would have been a much better place if Noah had refused to let the two mosquitoes board the Ark.

**38.** Why did the parrot wear a plastic raincoat?

Because it was starting to rain heavily so it wanted to be polyunsaturated.

**39.** If ants are always supposed to be so busy – how is it that they can spend so much time at picnics?

**40.** What is the difference between a puppy and a woman?

The puppy will soon grow up and stop whining.

**41.** The bat was very tired. It sunk lower and lower until it did not have enough energy to flap its wings any more and so it flopped to the ground.

After a few minutes it crawled along the grass until it came to the old trees where it lived. Then it suddenly raced towards the trees, stopped when it almost hit them, then went backwards. Then it raced towards the trees again.

It did this so many times that I became curious.

'Why are you racing towards the trees, stopping, going backwards, then racing towards them again?' I asked.

The bat sighed, then said (for it was a talking bat): 'I was very run down and so I needed to charge my bat-trees.'


**42.** Why were there so many bees in the toilet at the petrol station?

Because they saw the sign advertising BP.


**43.** The two birds met for the first time in a tree and one of them said, 'Bred any good rooks recently?'


**44.** Outraged customer: This cat you sold me is absolutely useless!

Petshop owner: What's wrong with it? It looks perfectly all right to me.

Outraged customer: When you sold it to me you promised it would be a good cat for mice. Yet every time it sees a mouse it runs away and hides.

Petshop owner: Well, isn't that a good cat for mice?


**45.** Our house is so small I had to train the dog to wag its tail up and down instead of from side to side.

**46.** One day I'd like to have enough courage to say to people who keep telling me that their pet dog is just like one of the family, 'Oh – which one is it like?'

**47.** Fred: We've got a new dog. Would you like to come and play with him?

Tom: I've heard him barking and growling. He sounds very fierce and unfriendly. Does he bite?

Fred: That's what I want to find out.

**48.** Timothy: I say, your dog is very clever being able to play the trombone.

Algernon: Not really – he can't read a single note of music.

**49.** Albert has got the laziest dog in the world. Even when he's watering his garden, the dog refuses to lift a leg to help.

**50.** 'What is your dog's name?'
    'I don't know. He refuses to tell me.'

**51.** My dog is a Dobermann pinscher. Every time he sees a Dobermann, he pinches it.

**52.** When Poole and Bournemouth introduced bye-laws to ban dogs from certain parts of the beach and to fine their owners if the dogs fouled public places, a friend of mine decided that she had better train her dog to go to the toilet in the gutter. This was rather difficult, as the dog kept falling off the roof.

**53.** A friend of mine keeps making films about canine creatures – they are all *dog*umentaries.

**54.** What noise do you get if you cross a cocker spaniel with a poodle and a cockerel?
   A cockerpoodledoo.

**55.** If animals are not supposed to be eaten, why are they made of meat?

**56.** I've just come from an awkward meeting with my next-door neighbour. He's almost seven feet tall and has a huge Alsatian dog.
   Unfortunately, the dog kept leaping at the garden fence so much that it made a hole in it and got into my garden. That was when it happened. My little cat killed the big Alsatian.
   'How did your puny cat kill Big Al, my dog?' demanded my neighbour.
   'I'm sorry,' I said, 'but my cat stuck in your dog's throat and he choked to death.'

**57.** Farmer Jim was very worried about the poor performance of his prize bull for which he had paid an astronomical sum. He talked to all his friends every time he went to the market and one day learned from a cousin that there was an amazing vet way down in the West Country.

He was so depressed about the bull that he decided this last resort was the answer and he took himself off to Cornwall to find the vet. At last he found the chap who urged him to give his bull a great big pill once a day.

A few months later he met his cousin who asked him how he had got on. 'Oh, it was marvellous,' he said. 'He gave me these pills for the bull and I had no sooner started him off on them when he hit the jackpot. In fact,' he said, 'I am making a fortune out of the local farmers – they can't get their cows round here fast enough!'

'What are these pills then?' asked his cousin.

'Oh!' said Farmer Jim, 'Huge great green jobs like bombs, with a peppermint taste!'

**58.** Wealthy poultry farmer, Bernard Nurnberg, of Tucson, Arizona was over in the UK on a turkey safari, looking for new ways to boost his production. He arrived at a small farm near Ballachulish and announced himself to the diminutive Scots farmer, Hamish McTavish:

'The name's Nurnberg, Bernard Nurnberg,' he warbled, shaking the Scotsman's hand vigorously. 'I'm here to find out how you raise turkeys right here in Scotland. How large is your farm?'

'Och well,' said Hamish, 'if you look down the burn on your left that is my left-hand boundary. Where you see the woods in the distance is my bottom boundary. Now here on the right-hand side is a wee "tump", as we call it in Scotland (which just means a small hill) and if you look where we have burnt the heather in a long line along the side of the hill, that is my right-hand boundary. The roadway where you have just come in completes the square so really, when you are standing here, you can see the lot.'

'Oh my,' drawled Bernard, 'compared to my estate in Arizona, this is just a side-show! Why back home it takes three days just to drive my truck around the perimeter!'

'Is *that* so?' rejoined Hamish, and after a thoughtful pause, 'It will be some years now I suppose, since *I* had a *truck* like that!'

**59.** One farmer I know is trying to cross a cow with an octopus. He wants to breed a creature that can milk itself.

**60.** My wife, Virginia, likes to talk to the plants in the garden. So far, only one of them talks back and is always saying things like, 'You're wonderful, beautiful. Thank you for looking after me in the garden. You're fantastic!'

I suppose this was only to be expected of a plant called Virginia Creeper!

**61.** My dog keeps making mistakes – he's a cock-up spaniel.

**62.** I once knew a rather ridiculous man who named his pet zebra 'Spot'.

**63.** Philosophy of a skunk: I stink, therefore I am.

**64.** For the summer Saturday outing to the park, the little girl put a small furry animal into a wicker basket – it was her picnic hamster.


**65.** 'Dad, can pies fly?'

'No, of course not, son.'

'But mum insists that there are two magpies flying around the garden.'


**66.** One of my cousins says he wants to take up pigeon racing – but I'm sure he'll never win against them unless he learns how to fly.


**67.** One of the healthiest animals in the zoo is the ant-eater. It's got lots of protection against diseases as it's full of anty-bodies.


**68.** The insomniac sheep could only get to sleep by counting people.


**69.** When the budgie got sick, my children insisted I took it to the vet for tweetment.


**70.** My young son came rushing into my study shouting, 'I've been stung! I've been stung by a wasp!'

'Don't worry,' I soothed. 'I'll put some special cream on it.'

'That's no good,' said my son, 'the wasp has flown away and you'll never find it.'

**71.** Farmer Giles went to the sales to buy himself a horse. Unfortunately, that day there were no horses but the final lot to come up was a zebra and even though he knew that no one had ever trained a zebra to do anything before, he decided to make a low offer. Naturally he got it. Knowing what he knew, he immediately told the zebra that when he got back to the farm he was to go around all the animals and chat to them about their work and then decide what he could do best. He warned the zebra that if he did not become a useful animal within six weeks he would be packed off to the abattoir.

So the zebra lost no time in talking to the animals. He asked the hen first what she did. 'Oh well,' cackled the hen, 'I peck around the farmyard here, pick up a few worms and as long as I lay an egg every day old Giles leaves me alone – it's a good life really.' 'I don't think I would like that,' said the zebra, 'I think I will go and talk to the pig and see what he does.'

He explained to the pig the stern command that he had had from Giles and asked him what he did. 'Oh I enjoy myself,' the pig snorted. 'I snuffle around in this mud and he gives me lots of hot potato peelings and good food and doesn't ask me for much. The only thing that worries me is that a few of my brothers have disappeared recently and I don't think what happens to them is terribly good news. Still, I live in the hope that my turn is yet a long way off.'

The zebra thought this was a little uncertain for him so he continued with his inquiries by asking the bull what he did for a living. The bull snorted impatiently, 'If you take those silly pyjamas off,' he roared, 'I will show you!'


**72.** The zoo had fallen on hard times. The numbers of visitors had fallen dramatically over the years and now the zoo was facing bankruptcy. It would have to close.

The zoo owners decided to sell all the animals and birds in the zoo at auction in an attempt to raise as much money as possible towards the zoo's debts.

Bidding was particularly good for one of the parrots. The auctioneer started the bidding at £100 and the price rapidly rose to £1,000 and the parrot was eventually sold to a young man for £1,250.

As the successful bidder wrote out a cheque, he said to the auctioneer's assistant, 'I think I got carried away with the excitement of it all. I didn't intend to pay all that much for the parrot, but as the price went up and up it seemed the bird must be really good. I hope that for £1,250 the parrot can talk a lot.'

'He certainly can,' said the auctioneer's assistant. 'Who do you think was bidding against you?'


**73.** The male gymnast needed to raise money to support himself while in training and to pay for his travel and hotel expenses during overseas competitions.

He was therefore delighted when he was asked to participate in a secret mission for a month during the peak tourist season at the local zoo.

The zoo's much loved ape had just died. It was a great tourist attraction as he was extremely acrobatic: jumping from branch to branch, swinging from ropes, doing somersaults. The zoo did not want to admit that the ape had died as many people came to the zoo just to watch the ape. Without such an attraction, the number of visitors would decline – and the zoo needed every paying customer it could get in order to survive.

The gymnast was therefore asked to dress up in the ape's skin and act like the ape: tumbling, swinging and being extremely energetic.

The gymnast loved this new work and all went well until the last week of the engagement. After a particularly energetic swing on the rope he accidentally let go and hurtled out of the cage and into the lion's enclosure.

As he landed, he looked up to see a fierce lion approaching. He started to scream for help, but the lion put a mighty paw across the gymnast's mouth and hissed, 'Sssh! Do you want us *both* to lose our summer jobs?'

**74.** Some of the animals in the zoo disliked being looked at by hordes of noisy visitors every day. They knew there was nothing they could do about their situation, but to pass away the time in their cramped cages and enclosures they would sometimes wonder what it would be like if they could take some revenge on their human tormentors.

'I'd like to eat that fat actor who is always bringing his stupid children to drop coins on my head in a feeble attempt to see if I'm awake or asleep,' said one of the crocodiles.

'I agree,' replied another crocodile, 'although as I'm Jewish I wouldn't be able to eat such ham. But there are other equally dreadful people whom I could cheerfully chomp.'

'So could I,' agreed a lion. 'But the tastiest meat would probably be that well-known politician. I'd love to give him one big bite to let all the wind out of him – then what was left would be delicious: soft, fleshy and absolutely no backbone.'

# BOOKS

**75.** The reason he doesn't read books by Tolkien is because he's afraid they might become hobbit-forming.

**76.** I was feeling rather stressed and tormented, so last night I read a book that stated that the way to achieve inner peace was to finish the things I started.

I'm now well on the way to feeling better. So far I've managed to finish a packet of cornflakes, a chocolate bar, a bottle of wine, a four-course lunch, two bags of peanuts, a large bag of potato chips and six cans of beer. I feel a great inner calm ...

**77.** She thought that *Pride and Prejudice* was a story about discrimination amongst a group of lions.

**78.** He's really excited. He's just been given a hard hitting book that's not afraid to name names – it's a telephone directory.

**79.** What do you get if you throw a copy of *The Canterbury Tales* in the air?

A flying Chaucer.

**80.** What was enormous, very heavy, lived a long time ago and liked *Wuthering Heights* and *Jane Eyre*?
  A Bronte-saurus.


**81.** My next book is about two families who constantly fight and argue – it's a book of friction!


**82.** My books of prose may be bad, but they could be verse.


**83.** I once knew an author who changed his name to Biro because he wanted a pen name.


**84.** The world's shortest book contained no words. Its title was: *All I Know About Women*.


**85.** *Is It In The Stars?* by Zoe D Ack.


**86.** *Great Eggspectations* by Charles Chickens.


**87.** *In The Soup* by Minni Stroney.


**88.** *How Sherlock Holmes Quickly Solved Crimes* by L M N Tree.


**89.** *Big Celebrations* by Annie Versary.

# BUSINESS & WORK

**90.** The very busty accountant's assistant can't add. But she can certainly distract.

**91.** He's such a good accountant he has a tax loophole named after him.

**92.** What do accountants suffer from that other people do not? Depreciation.

**93.** The trouble with the auditing profession is that 95 per cent of its members give the others a bad name.

**94.** Unfortunately, he lost his left arm, left ear and left leg in an industrial accident. He's all right now.

**95.** Luke and Charles earned a fortune in the City working for rival merchant banks. They had known each other for several years and occasionally had dinner together at an extremely expensive restaurant, charging the bill to their employers.

After one such meal, as they were leaving the restaurant, Charles almost trod in some dog muck.

'I bet you wouldn't dare pick a bit up and eat it,' said Luke.

'Don't be disgusting!' replied Charles. 'You must be drunk. Anyway, what would you bet?'

'£150,000,' said Luke.

Charles thought about the offer. He knew that Luke could well afford the bet, so said: 'OK I'll do it.'

Charles picked up a tiny bit of the dog mess, put it in his mouth and swallowed quickly. 'Yuk!' he said, as Luke took out his cheque book and gave him a cheque. A short while later, they encountered another pile of dog muck. Charles looked at Luke and said: 'I bet you £150,000 that you won't eat a bit of that muck.'

'You're on,' said Luke, bending down and picking up a small amount of dog muck and swallowing it down. When Charles handed Luke a cheque, Luke said: 'You know. We've both eaten disgusting dog muck tonight. And I can't see that either of us is any better off.'

'Of course we are!' said Charles. 'We've just done £300,000 worth of trade.'

**96.** When he went to the bank and asked the cashier to check his balance she asked him to stand on one leg and said she'd time how long he could remain like that.

**97.** James is rather suspicious of his boss. Whenever he sees James he thumps him on the back, supposedly in welcome. James says it feels more like his back is being treated like meat – tenderised before a knife gets plunged into it.

**98.** Clare was talking to her friend, Fiona. 'I'm really worried. I just don't know what I'm going to do.'

'What's wrong?' asked Fiona.

'It's my boss,' said Clare. 'He says he's paying too much rent.'

'How does that concern you?' asked Fiona.

'Because,' replied Clare, 'in return for a special service, it's the rent on my apartment he's paying.'

**99.** His boss fired him, saying: 'You've been like a son to me – lazy, disrespectful and always whining for more money.'

**100.** I've no idea what makes my boss tick – but I certainly know what makes him explode.

**101.** He's a very tough boss. If you get something wrong he likes to shout and bawl and inflict mental torture. Indeed, his motto is: If at first you don't succeed then try, try, try more pain.

**102.** My boss used to be indecisive – now he's not so sure.

**103.** My boss urgently needs a heart transplant, but the surgeons are having difficulty finding a suitable one. It's not often they have to get one made of stone.

**104.** The chief executive of a bankrupt high tech company was facing a stormy meeting of his investors.

'I invested over five million in your firm and I've lost the lot!' said one outraged man. 'What have you got to say for yourself?'

'I'm sorry,' replied the chief executive, 'but it could have been much worse.'

Another investor said, 'My fund management firm invested over fifty million with your firm – and then subscribed to a rights issue which cost us another fifty million. Aren't you ashamed?'

'Of course,' replied the chief executive, 'but it could have been worse.'

A portly gentleman in a pin-stripe suit stood up and said, 'I'm appalled by the way you ran the company into the ground while taking a fat salary with lots of other benefits. My group of investment companies has lost well over two hundred million. You ...'

The chief executive raised a calming hand and said, 'I'm genuinely sorry, but I think it could have been worse.'

An elderly lady shouted, 'I lost half my pension investing it in your firm. And apart from saying sorry you keep saying "It could have been worse". We've all suffered great financial loss – so how could it have been worse?'

The chief executive replied, 'Instead of raising money from shareholders I could have invested my *own* money in the company.'

**105.** He always tried to pay his bills with a smile. The problem was that his creditors wanted cash.

**106.** He started his business career in the mailroom of a large company. Within a month he had been promoted to assistant office manager. Two months later he was office manager. After only three months in that position he was appointed as a director of the company. As he entered the room for his first board meeting he looked at the chairman and said: 'Hello, Dad.'

**107.** The British government ordered the Civil Service to cut red tape. The Civil Service responded by cutting it lengthways so they could wrap even more things in it.

**108.** Why is a senior civil servant like a broken gun?
Because when it doesn't work you can't fire it.

**109.** 'Foolproof' when applied to certain computer software usually means 'proof it was designed by a fool'.

**110.** Why is it that computer programs always seem to become obsolete just after you've learnt how to use them?

**111.** Humans are better than computers because humans are easier to maintain and it doesn't need much intelligence to make one.

**112.** Somehow I don't think he'll be offered the job for which he has applied. At the bottom of the application form, where it stated 'Sign here', he wrote 'Capricorn'.

**113.** The rebels had moved into the holiday resort and captured three men: a management consultant and two salesmen.
The captives were taken to the rebel headquarters where they were to be held hostage until the government gave in to their demands.

Unfortunately, the government refused to comply with the rebels' requests so the three men were told they would be executed, but they could choose the method: firing squad or guillotine.

All three chose the guillotine, believing it would be the fastest and most painless end. Many members of the rebel army seemed to be hooked on drugs and the firing squad's aim might not be too accurate and the captured men might just be badly injured and slowly bleed to death.

The first salesman was brought to the guillotine. He knelt down with his head in the correct position – and the blade came down – but stopped before it could cut his neck.

'This is a sign from God,' said the salesman. 'He does not want me to be killed. You should set me free.' He then went on in great detail about how he would promote the rebels' cause to the outside world. The rebel leader agreed to let him go.

One of the rebels re-adjusted the guillotine and the second salesman was forced into position. The blade came hurtling down – but stopped before it reached him.

'Another sign from God,' shouted the salesman. 'You should free me. Not only will I promote your cause I can raise money for you, too.'

The rebel leader agreed to let him go.

Then the management consultant was led towards the guillotine, but he shouted: 'Stop! That thing clearly does not work properly. You'd better use the firing squad instead.'

**114.** He was telling his wife how good his colleague was at the office. 'He's so helpful – I'd trust him with my life.' 'But,' she said, 'would you trust him with anything of great value?'

**115.** He didn't go to work yesterday because he was sick. He was sick of work.

**116.** She used to file her nails in the office – in the large grey filing cabinet under 'N'.

**117.** Trains stop at a train station. Buses stop at a bus station. So why should I act differently in the office at my work station?

**118.** Bill asked his friend Philip to buy a raffle ticket.

'What's the raffle for?' asked Philip.

'You know Fred in accounts?' asked Bill. Philip nodded.

Bill continued: 'Fred and his wife died in a car crash last week so the raffle is for his children.'

'Why,' asked Philip, 'would I want to buy such a raffle ticket? I'm already supporting three children of my own – I certainly don't want to win any more.'

**119.** One door-to-door vacuum cleaner salesman consistently beat all sales records. His boss therefore decided to accompany the salesman to see what sales techniques he was using in the hope of being able to persuade others to use them.

The first door the salesman knocked on was opened by a middle-aged woman. 'Good morning,' said the salesman, 'Yesterday I visited one of your neighbours and I was demonstrating this vacuum cleaner when she told me a lot of interesting gossip. Would you like me to come in and tell you what she said?'

**120.** Yesterday a man knocked on my door and tried to sell me a lawn mower. I told him to visit my neighbour instead – I'm always borrowing his mower and it's time he got a better one I could borrow.

**121.** The salesman believed that to find out if honesty was the best policy he had to try all the other options first.

**122.** I recently went on a stress management course. Now I fully understand the real cause of stress – it's management.

**123.** A woman who wants to be as successful as a man is a woman who lacks real ambition.

**124.** The reason so few women break through the glass ceiling is because they know they'll get no help from men to pick up the pieces.

**125**. The company personnel department had carefully interviewed thirty-eight people for the job of assistant to the financial director.

The chief executive thought that one candidate – Charles – seemed ideal. Charles had been to a major public school. Not only was he a qualified accountant, but Charles also had a masters degree in business administration. He seemed fully aware of the latest creative accountancy techniques.

'Charles,' said the chief executive, 'we've decided to offer you the job. And as you're so well qualified we've decided to start you off on a slightly higher salary than the one advertised. We'll pay you £48,000 a year.'

'Thank you,' replied Charles. 'But how much is that per month?'

**126.** The tired, exhausted businessman had felt compelled to drink more than he could really cope with at a business lunch at which he had lost his firm's major client.

The businessman staggered back to the office and asked his gorgeous secretary, 'Can you give me something to ease my pain?'

'How about something tall and cold?' replied the secretary.

'Don't!' said the businessman. 'Don't bring my wife into it.'

**127.** When I asked my boss for a salary rise because I was doing the work of three men, he said he couldn't increase my pay but, if I told him the names of the three men, he'd fire them.

**128.** I'm always delighted when people stick their noses in my business – my company makes paper tissues.

**129.** My husband's business is rather up-and-down – he makes yo-yos.

**130.** When Bernard got fired from his last job they were really tough. They made him hand back his keys to the executive toilets, return his company credit card, give back his company car, and even give back his ulcer!

**131.** Last night I discovered why my boss hired *me* to be his deputy rather than all the other candidates. Over a lengthy business dinner he admitted that when he interviewed all the other candidates, they seemed to be the cleverest, most dynamic people in the world.

Yet when he interviewed me, I managed to convince him that *he* was the cleverest, most dynamic person in the world.


**132.** A friend of mine is a very successful businessman. He started with £5,000 – now he owes £55 million.


**133.** I once knew a man who was always travelling abroad for business. One trip lasted two whole months and towards the end of it he could stand it no longer and went to the local brothel.

'I would like your most bored, tired, fat lady,' he said.

'Why do you want someone like that?' asked the surprised madam.

'Because,' replied the businessman, 'I've been away for so long I'm homesick for my wife!'


**134.** I once knew a couple who were in the iron and steel business – she did the ironing, while he went out stealing.


**135.** To all those people who keep telling me that 'hard work never hurt anyone', I would just like to ask, 'Name anyone who got hurt because they *didn't* do hard work.'


**136.** My employer is the sort of man who grows on you – like warts.

**137.** The managing director of a large company – which he had founded – received a short job application letter for the position of assistant managing director from a young man who detailed his education at a top public school, outlined his aristocratic background and intentions of marrying the daughter of a duke – yet failed to give any indication of his competency or even knowledge of the job available.

The managing director therefore felt obliged to write back to the young man: 'Dear Sir, Thank you for applying for the position advertised. I am unable to employ you since we require the services of someone for managerial rather than breeding purposes.'

**138.** Boss: I don't like 'yes' men. When I say 'no' I want them to say 'no' too.

**139.** My boss is so mean that whenever he pays anyone a compliment he insists on a receipt.

**140.** We don't know what to get our boss for Christmas. What do you get for someone who's had everybody?

**141.** There's a man in my office whose nickname is Caterpillar – because he's always crawling.

**142.** The young student was desperate for money and so in his vacation he decided to take a job in a local factory as it paid good wages.

'Now,' said the supervisor, 'your first job is to sweep the floor.'

'But I've got a BA degree,' said the student, 'and I'm currently studying for a masters in business administration.'

'Oh!' said the supervisor. 'In that case, I'd better show you how to hold the broom.'

**143.** My wife is thinking of applying for a job as a telephone canvasser – she says she'll enjoy making little tents for telephones.

**144.** A friend of mine is very pleased with his wife. He thinks she's got a good part-time job with a London law firm, working two evenings each week. But all she told him was that to get money for a few extra luxuries, she would now be soliciting in Paddington.

**145.** My sister has a very responsible job. If anything goes wrong, she's responsible.

**146.** The best job for people who think they are paranoid is driving a taxi – then they really will always have people talking behind their backs.

**147.** My job is very secure – it's *me* they can do without.

**148.** When I left university I went for several job interviews. At the first interview I was turned down because I wasn't married. The personnel officer said that married men had much more experience of knowing how to cope if a boss shouted at them.

**149.** Why do I have to work so much overtime at the office?

Because I owe, I owe, so off to work I go.

**150.** The new office boy was bitterly denying to his older colleague that he was a crawler: 'It's not true that I lick my boss's shoes every day – he's only in the office on Mondays and Thursdays.'

**151.** The young office girl was about to get married. Her colleagues made a collection and bought her a wedding present.

'Where shall we hide it until the boss can present it to her?' asked one of her colleagues.

Just then the boss appeared, 'I heard that,' he said. 'Just put the present in a filing cabinet – she never seems capable of finding anything in there!'

**152.** 'Simpkins, how many people work in your office?'

'About half of them, sir.'

**153.** I once went to an important business dinner party and was listening to an interesting conversation between two people at the far end of the table when the host (my boss) passed me a note.

I had forgotten to bring my spectacles, so I handed the note to the man on my right and asked him if he would be kind enough to read me the note as, without my spectacles, I find it difficult even to read newspaper headlines.

The young man looked at the note and read, 'Please talk to the man on your right. He's a long-winded bore, full of his own self-importance and is rather stupid – but we're hoping to pick up a good order from his firm.'

**154.** There I was at the office cocktail party. I'd spent a small fortune on a new suit and my wife had spent even more on her dress.

I wanted to impress my new boss, but my wife seemed to be letting me down. Every five minutes or so she would go over to the bar and get a drink and bring it back to where I was standing, and then rapidly drink it with her back to the bar.

By the time she had finished her seventh drink I noticed that my boss was watching her as she made her way back to the bar.

I wanted to go after my wife, but it was difficult to break off the conversation I was having with someone from the IT department. Out of the corner of my eye I could see my boss talking to my wife. He smiled. She smiled. He frowned. Then she walked back to me.

'Darling,' I said to my wife, when the IT man had moved on to buttonhole someone else, 'what did my boss say to you? Did he comment on all the drinks you've had? That won't do my career much good. He must think you've got a drink problem.'

'No, he doesn't,' replied my wife. 'He certainly doesn't think I've got a drink problem. I'm *not* a liability to you, darling. I simply told him you just keep sending me to the bar to get more drinks for you.'

**155.** I used to be a private detective. I once had to follow a woman from London to Bournemouth, where she gave me the slip.

Another time I managed to follow her to Newcastle, where she again gave me the slip.

Then I followed her to London where she gave me the slip.

Then I got lucky. When I followed her to York she not only gave me the slip – but her bra and panties, too!

**156.** When Simpkins-Smutterwhite was promoted above me – even though I had been with the company for much longer, had more experience and worked much harder than he did – I was not upset. I went straight up to him and said, 'Congratulations! Let me shake you by the throat.'

**157.** One door-to-door salesman does very well by using the opening line, 'Can I interest you in something your neighbour said you couldn't possibly afford?'

**158.** 'Humpkins!' boomed the boss. 'When I told you to fire the salesmen with enthusiasm, I did *not* want you to sack them all enthusiastically!'

**159.** The only orders the new trainee door-to-door salesman got were 'go away' and 'get out'.

**160.** The sweet young secretary is busy applying make-up when the phone rings. She picks it up and a voice asks, 'Is Mr Schwartz in yet?'
'No,' replies the secretary, 'he hasn't even been in yesterday yet.'

**161.** My secretary has only been working for me for two weeks and already she's a month behind.

**162.** Senior civil servant: Did you phone my wife as I asked you to?

Secretary: Certainly, sir. I told her you would be late home from the office due to an unexpected conference.

Senior civil servant: And what did she say?

Secretary: Can I rely on that?


**163.** Secretary to an irate gentleman on the phone, 'Oh! Didn't you get our letter – I'm about to post it now.'


**164.** When I arrived for work this morning, my secretary said, 'I can see you've had another quarrel with your wife.'
  'Oh,' I said, rather stunned. 'How did you know that?'
  'Because,' she replied, 'the kitchen knife is still stuck in your back.'


**165.** The young secretary, Dawn, used to tell such long, complicated and involved jokes to her colleagues in the office that they were often to be found asleep at the crack of Dawn.


**166.** I once said to my delightful young secretary, 'I just don't know what to do. What can I give to a valued client – a man who has expensive cars, an art collection worth millions, homes in London, Dorset, Switzerland and the USA. He's a man with just about everything. What can I possibly give him?'
  My secretary looked at me, smiled, and said, 'You're welcome to give him my phone number.'

**167.** My new secretary seems to think that all my correspondence is private and confidential: all the letters she types look as if she's taken them down in shorthand and typed them while wearing a blindfold.

**168.** His secretary is a miracle worker – it's a miracle if she works.

**169.** I recently had to fire my secretary for pulling funny faces – the people didn't like it when she grabbed them and pulled their faces.

**170.** My new secretary seems to like wearing clothes that bring out the bust in her.

**171.** Secretary: Please, Mr Jenkins, can I have two weeks off work?

Mr Jenkins: What for?

Secretary: I'm getting married.

Mr Jenkins: But you've only just returned from your three-week summer holiday? Why didn't you get married then?

Secretary: What? And ruin my summer holiday!

**172.** Mrs Jones: I'm Mr Jones's wife.

Beautiful young secretary: Are you? I'm his secretary.

Mrs Jones: *Were* you?


**173.** Now I work for myself I find the greatest difficulty is that when I phone to say I'm sick I don't know whether to believe myself.


**174.** One trade union is now demanding that unskilled workers get paid more than skilled workers because the work is harder if people are not skilled to do it.


**175.** Then there was the trade union leader who used to tell bedtime stories to his children: 'Once upon a double time ...'


**176.** He likes to do things right the first time. But he deliberately doesn't do it too often. He says he wants people to really appreciate that his work is very difficult.

# CHILDREN & SCHOOL

**177.** Teacher: Now, Susan, can you tell me where God lives?

Susan: Miss, I think he lives in the bathroom.

Teacher: In the bathroom! Why do you think that?

Susan: Because every morning, I can hear my father knock on the bathroom door and say, 'God, are you still in there?'

**178.** The young boy was boasting that he knew all the capitals, so I asked him, 'What is the capital of Iceland?' 'That's easy,' he said. 'It's I.'

**179.** He was very annoyed when his young son staggered home pushing an old pram with two chairs and a sofa precariously balanced on it. 'How many times do I have to tell you?' asked the father. 'You should never take suites from strangers!'

**180.** When eight-year-old Jonathan came home from school his mother said, 'Daddy would like to see you in his study.'
  'Oh no!' said Jonathan. 'I don't want to go in there.'

'Why not?' asked his mother. 'You've done nothing wrong. He just wants a little chat with you.'

Reluctantly, Jonathan entered his father's study.

'Sit down,' said his father. 'I think you're old enough for me to tell you about the birds and the bees.'

Jonathan screamed, 'No! No!' and put his hands over his ears.

His father went to calm him down. 'What's the matter?' he gently asked.

'I don't like hearing things in your study,' replied Jonathan. 'When I was smaller and you first asked me to come in here, you told me there was no such thing as Santa Claus. The next time you asked me to your study, you told me there was no tooth fairy. And if you're now going to tell me there's no such thing as sex, then I don't want to hear it.'


**181.** 'Why are you staring at that carton of orange juice?' asked Mavis.

'Because,' replied her son, 'on the carton it says *Concentrate*.'


**182.** When a child is born its parents spend the first eighteen months of the child's life encouraging it to talk and walk. The next eighteen months they spend telling the child to shut up and sit down.


**183.** John kept racing around the house shouting, 'Cluck, cluck, cluck.' His parents told him to stop using fowl language.


**184.** Lionel had been very good during his grandmother's visit. He was polite and his table manners were impeccable. After a week of such excellent behaviour,

Lionel asked, 'Grandma, when are you going to give the climbing lessons?' The grandmother looked puzzled. 'Climbing lessons?' she asked. 'What do you mean?'

'Well,' said Lionel, 'Dad said that if you stayed more than a week you would have him climbing the walls.'


**185.** His wife was very pleased with her son's report from school. It stated the son was making excellent progress for a ten-year-old. Her husband doesn't share his wife's views – the son is sixteen.


**186.** He was sitting in the kitchen reading a newspaper when he saw his young son boiling water in a kettle, then letting it cool down, then boiling it again.

'What on earth are you doing?' he asked his son.

'Oh, Dad,' said the son. 'I need to boil and re-boil the water lots of times. I'm trying to make holy water – but to do that I need to boil the Hell out of it.'


**187.** When her daughter came home from school and asked, 'Mum, do you know anything about the Dead Sea?'

She replied, 'No – I didn't even know about it when it was ill.'


**188.** During a thunderstorm the small boy told his mother that he was frightened by the lightning. His mother put her arms around him and said, 'Don't worry. It will be over in a flash.'


**189.** I have a young nephew who refuses to play on the lawn. He says it's dangerous as grass has blades.

**190.** When I told my young son to eat up his spinach so that he would grow up to be big and strong like Popeye, he said: 'What? And end up with a girlfriend who looks like Olive Oyl?'

**191.** When I asked my young nephew if he could tell me what a beeline is, he told me it was the distance between two buzz stops.

**192.** When his computer teacher asked him to give an example of software he suggested a velvet jacket.

**193.** Kids these days are so into computers that when I gave one of my nephews a book for Christmas he spent two hours trying to find where to plug it in.

**194.** As a small boy I used to like maths until we had to do algebra. To me, it was a weapon of *math* destruction.

**195.** The school teacher asked: 'How many days of the week start with the letter "T"?'

Clarissa eagerly put up her hand and said, 'Two, miss.'

'That's right,' said the teacher. 'Very good. Now can you tell me the names of those two days that start with a T?'

'Of course,' replied Clarissa. 'Today and Tomorrow.'

**196.** 'Now,' said the school teacher, 'who can tell me what it means if you find a horseshoe?'

Christy put up her hand and said, 'I can, miss. If you find a horseshoe it means a poor horse is having to limp. On one of its feet it has only got a sock.'

**197.** The school teacher asked James, 'How many letters are there in the alphabet?'

James replied, 'Eleven.'

Puzzled, the teacher asked, '*Why* do you think the alphabet only has eleven letters?'

'Easy,' replied James. 'T.H.E. A.L.P.H.A.B.E.T. – that's eleven letters.'

**198.** The teacher began the lesson by saying, 'Rotting food, take-away cartons, empty boxes, used tissues, broken bottles, crumpled cardboard ...'

'Oh dear,' whispered one pupil to her friend, 'He's talking garbage again.'

**199.** I'm fed up with school,' said Emily. 'How do the teachers expect us to learn when they can never make up their minds.'

'What do you mean?' asked Emily's mother.

'On Monday,' said Emily, 'the teacher told us that two plus seven makes nine. Then on Tuesday she said that three plus six makes nine. And today she *still* wasn't sure of the right answer as she said five plus four makes nine.'

**200.** When the teacher asked John to recite his tables he said: 'Dining table, coffee table, bedside table and kitchen table.'

**201.** A schoolteacher asked my young cousin: 'If you had £8.70 in one pocket and £9.30 in another pocket, what would you have?'

My cousin replied: 'Someone else's clothes.'

**202.** He was so unpopular at school that when he played hide-and-seek no one came to find him.

**203.** When Claude's wife was expecting their second child he told his three-year-old son that soon a giant stork would be arriving and it would land on the chimney of their house. In the stork's beak would be a wonderful present.

'Oh,' said Claude's son, 'I hope it will be quiet and won't upset mummy. A giant bird suddenly arriving like that might give her a shock. And that wouldn't be any good as you know you made her pregnant and she's expecting a baby.'

**204.** Dorothy: Mum, did you know that Marconi was a famous inventor.

Mother: Yes, dear. But it's not polite to say Ma Coni – you should say Mrs Coni.

**205.** Yesterday, my young daughter (we called her 'Yesterday' because she was an afterthought) asked my husband, 'Where do I come from?'

He was rather embarrassed, so he told her to ask me.

'Where do I come from?' she asked again, and so I carefully explained to her all about love, marriage, sex, all the facts of life.

My daughter then said, 'Yes, I know all that. But where do I come from? My friend Sally comes from Cardiff – where do *I* come from?'

**206.** This morning my son asked me if I could tell him what makes the sky blue. I told him to look it up in an encyclopedia.

At lunchtime he asked me how long it would take to boil an ostrich egg. I said I didn't know.

This afternoon my son asked me how far away from Earth is the planet Mars. I said I didn't know.

Earlier this evening he asked me how deep a fathom is in metres. I said I didn't know, but he could look it up on the internet.

Just before I left to come to this meeting, my son asked me, 'Who was the first King of England?' I said I couldn't remember.

Then he asked me, 'Do you mind me asking you so many questions?'

I told him, 'Of course not.' After all, how else will he learn things if he doesn't ask questions?

**207.** My youngest son thinks that a wombat is a thing you use to play wom.

**208.** I once overhead a small girl talking to one of her friends: 'The way mummies and daddies and teachers are always moaning and groaning no wonder they are called *groan*-ups.'

**209.** My small son showed me this morning how to make a cigarette lighter. He took most of the tobacco out of it.

**210.** 'Mum,' asked the small girl, 'do you mind if my exam results are like a submarine?'

'What do you mean?' asked the mother.

'Below C-level.'

**211.** My daughter walks very quietly whenever she's near the bathroom cabinet. She says she doesn't want to wake the sleeping pills.

**212.** My small son went with some friends to the local ice rink. When he returned, he told me, 'I still don't know if I can skate. I can't seem to stand upright long enough to find out.'

**213.** It was a tough neighbourhood. Two girls, Chantelle and Tracey were arguing:

'*My* mother is better than *your* mother,' shouted Chantelle.

'And *my* father is better than *your* father,' snapped Tracey.

'Oh,' said Chantelle. 'I suppose he is. Even my mum says so.'

**214.** I was sitting on a crowded train from Bournemouth to Waterloo when a young woman with her five children got on at Southampton. The children were all eating ice creams.

The train was so crowded there was nowhere to sit, so they stood in the narrow aisle and one of the children's ice creams kept touching the expensive fur coat of one of the seated passengers.

'Bernard!' snapped the child's mother. 'Don't hold your ice cream like that. You're getting bits of fur stuck in it.'

**215.** The children where I live are so sophisticated that when they write rude words on walls, they write them in ancient Greek and Latin.

**216.** Rebecca was going on safari in Africa with her parents during her summer holiday from school. She had to have the usual round of injections some weeks before her trip.

'Please can you put a plaster on my right arm?' Rebecca asked the nurse.

'Why?' said the nurse. 'You're right-handed and so I'm giving you the injections on your left arm. Why do you want a plaster on your right arm?'

'Because,' replied Rebecca, 'I have to go back to school after you've given me the injections.'

'I know,' said the nurse. 'That's why if you have the plaster over your injection on your left arm the other children at school will know you've had an injection and so will not bang or bump into your left arm.'

'If you knew the children in my school,' said Rebecca, 'you'd know that is *exactly* why I want the plaster on the wrong arm.'

**217.** Wilbur had just returned from an overseas business trip and staggered home with a large, brightly wrapped parcel. He was met at the door by his five children.

'Daddy,' asked one of the children, 'what's in the parcel?'

'It's a wonderful new toy,' replied Wilbur. 'It was given to me by one of my firm's clients. The problem is, he only gave me one toy, and as there are five of you, I don't know which one of you should have the toy.'

'Can't we share it?' asked one of the children.

'I suppose you could,' agreed Wilbur, 'but it's something that can only be played with by one person at a time, so I need to work out which one of you gets to use it first. Now, which person in the family always does as Mum tells them and never answers back?'

One of the children immediately responded, 'Daddy, you'd better have first go with the toy, then.'

**218.** My wife recently asked me if it was possible for a six-year-old boy to perform heart transplant operations.

'Of course it's not possible,' I replied.

'Jonathan,' shouted my wife. 'Daddy says you can't possibly do the operations. So go and put the hearts back right now!'

**219.** When the teacher asked him, 'What is a bar chart?', the little boy replied, 'A graph showing the decibel level of the voices of sheep.'

**220.** When I was a boy at school and studying biology the teacher suddenly picked on me and said, 'Boy! Why is mother's milk better than other milk?'

I was so flustered that all I could think of to say was, 'Mother's milk comes in more attractive containers.'

**221.** 'Brian,' said the kindergarten teacher, 'I know you like nursery rhymes so I'm sure you can tell me why the cow jumped over the moon.'

Brian thought for a moment, then said, 'Was it because the milkmaid had icy cold hands?'


**222.** 'Susan!' said the teacher. 'Why did you just let out that awful yell?'

'Please miss,' said Susan, 'I've just hit my fumb wiv a 'ammer.'

'Susan,' responded the teacher, 'the word is "thumb", not "fumb".'

'Yes miss,' said Susan, 'but as well as 'itting my thumb I also 'it my thinger.'


**223.** Teacher: When I was your age, I could name all the Presidents of America in the right order.

Jason: Sir, was that because when you were my age there had only been two or three Presidents?


**224.** 'Dad, I only got one question wrong in the maths exam at school today,' said the small boy.

'That's good,' replied the father. 'How many questions were there?'

'30.'

'You did very well to get 29 right.'

'Not really,' said the son, 'I couldn't answer 29 of them at all.'


**225.** When I went knocking on doors asking for donations for a new school swimming pool, one peculiar person gave me a bucket of water.

**226.** The little girl was accused of cheating during the biology examination – the teacher found her counting her breasts.

**227.** Teacher: Can you stand on your head?

Pupil: No. I can't get my feet up high enough.

**228.** Teacher: Now, Sarah, can you tell me what a skeleton is?

Sarah: Yes, sir! A skeleton is a set of bones with the person scraped off.

**229.** Teacher: If you stood facing due south, your back was north, what would be on your right hand?

Schoolgirl: Fingers.

**230.** Teacher: How many sheep does it take to make a man's jersey?

Small boy: I don't know. I didn't know sheep could knit.

**231.** What tickets did the babies sell at the school summer fête?
   Rattle tickets.

**232.** The small boy in the school in China was surprised when his teacher suddenly loomed over him and demanded, 'Are you chewing gum?'

'No,' replied the small boy, 'I'm Chiu N Fung.'

**233.** Teacher: Wendy, can you put 'defeat', 'deduct', 'defence' and 'detail' in a sentence?

Wendy: Yes, miss. De feet of de duck gets under de fence before de tail.

**234.** A friend of mine has a 15-year-old son at school in London. She's very worried about his progress. Although his teacher gave him an A in multi-cultural assimilation, an A in psycho-social awareness and another A in organizational behaviourism – my friend wonders when her son is going to learn how to read and write.

**235.** In the lesson, the biology teacher asked, 'What is a blood count?'

John promptly replied, 'Is it Count Dracula?'

**236.** I used to have a teacher at school who kept going on and on, insisting that 5 kilos of feathers weighed the same as 5 kilos of lead. So one day I emptied a 5 kilo bag of feathers over his head and then dropped a 5 kilo bag of lead on him. He was rather quiet after that.

**237.** Teacher: Samantha, where did you learn to swim so well?

Samantha: In the water.


**238.** Teacher: Now, Robert, can you tell me the name of a bird that cannot fly?

Robert: A roast chicken, sir.


**239.** Teacher: Simon, did your parents help you with this homework?

Simon: No, miss – I got it wrong all by myself this time.


**240.** The little boy on his first visit to the zoo followed all the signs. He saw the sign which said 'To the Elephants' and enjoyed watching them, then followed the sign 'To the Penguins' and found their antics amusing; but when he followed the sign 'To the Exit', he was disappointed at finding himself back in the street outside the zoo without seeing the Exit animal.

# CHRISTMAS

**241.** Santa Claus was fed up. His wife was continually nagging him. He had a bad cold. Several of his reindeer had run off. The sacks of toys kept bursting. And his little helpers had gone on strike. Suddenly, his doorbell rang. Opening the door he saw a small person dressed as an angel. 'I've brought a Christmas tree for you,' said the angel in a high-pitched, irritating voice. 'May you be full of the joys of Christmas. Where do you want me to put the tree?'

And this was how, due to a stressed-out Santa, that the tradition began of fixing a little angel to the top of the Christmas tree.

**242.** What do you call Santa's Christmas helpers?
Subordinate Clauses.

**243.** Every Christmas I get an awful pain that stays for a week. Then my mother-in-law goes back to her own home.

**244.** 'Mummy,' said the small boy, 'can I have a saluki or a dachshund for Christmas?'

'No,' replied his mother, 'you'll have what lots of other people are having – turkey.'

**245.** The little girl would have bought her grandmother a box of handkerchiefs for Christmas, but she couldn't do this as she said she didn't know the exact size of her grandmother's nose.

**246.** What do angry mice send at Christmas?
Cross mouse cards.

**247.** I once gave my boyfriend a pocket comb for Christmas, but he never used it. He said he didn't need to comb his pockets.

**248.** My husband is always moaning at me. Whatever I do, he can find something to complain about.

Last Christmas he gave me two pairs of ear-rings – one covered in plastic pearls and the other in fake diamonds.

When I put on the plastic pearl ones he said, 'What's wrong with the diamond ones. Don't you like them?'

**249.** I can always tell what my wife is getting me for Christmas by looking at our credit card statement.

# CLOTHES & FASHION

**250.** In the USA people have a legal right to wear shortsleeved clothes in the office and anywhere else. The Constitution protects their right to bare arms.

**251.** His parents had a passion for designer clothes. When he was a baby, people would tickle him under the chin and coo: 'Gucci, Gucci, goo.'

**252.** Wendy's mother came home one day having bought a fur coat.

'Mum, how *could* you?' asked Wendy, looking at the coat with anguish. 'Some poor dumb beast has had to *suffer* so that you could have that coat.'

Wendy's mother snapped: 'How *dare* you call your father a dumb beast!'

**253.** She's just bought a sheepdog bra. It was given that name because it rounds them up and points them in the right direction.

**254.** My wife was looking at an expensive dress. She turned to me and said, 'If I wore that dress I'm sure it would make me look years younger.'

'I know, dear,' I replied. 'But do you really want to look years *older* every time you take it off?'

**255.** His clothes look quite good considering the shape they're on.


**256.** I wouldn't say he was stupid – but he recently took a necktie back to the shop he bought it from. He told the store assistant he was returning the tie because it was too tight.

# COMPÈRES

**257.** 'Now we have that fantastic lady singer who got to the top because her dresses don't.'

**258.** 'Tonight, our rock group will sing a medley of their hit.'

**259.** 'There's always a long queue of people at his performances – trying to get out.'

**260.** 'We were going to have Morris Dancing – but Morris couldn't come.'

**261.** 'This evening, one of the beautiful chorus girls was hammering on my dressing-room door for more than fifty minutes . . . but I wouldn't let her out.'

**262.** 'He's just come from playing Julius Caesar. Caesar lost.'

**263.** 'Our next singer lacks only two things to get to the top: talent and ambition.'

**264.** 'Our next musician was even musical as a baby – he played on the linoleum.'

**265.** 'The last time he performed his act was right after the chimpanzees' tea party, and everyone thought it was an encore.'

**266.** 'Now we have a country singer. He has to sing in the country as they don't want him in the town.'

**267.** 'Next we have a group who will make you want to stamp your feet . . . all over them.'

**268.** 'I see there's a very posh lady in the front row of the audience tonight. She's eating her chips with her gloves on.'

**269.** 'Thank you for that amazing round of indifference.'

**270.** 'Our next singer is someone who wanted his name up in lights in every theatre in the world – so he changed his name to Exit.'

**271.** 'Our next comedian is so bad that when he took part in an open air show in the park 23 trees got up and walked out.'

**272.** 'Unfortunately, the actor who was to have been with us tonight has died. He caught a severe cold but, as you know, there's no curing an old ham.'

**273.** 'Now I'd like to introduce someone who, ten years ago, was an unknown failure. Now he's a famous failure.'

**274.** 'The next act are currently riding on the crest of a slump and I'm sure you'll be completely underwhelmed by them.'

**275.** 'I see we've got a very polite audience here tonight – they cover their mouths when they yawn.'

**276.** 'Now we have someone who has been practising the violin for twenty years – it was only last week that he discovered that you don't blow it.'

**277.** 'Our next lady singer is wearing a very nice dress. I wonder when that style will be in fashion again.'

**278.** 'Our next act will probably be up to our usual sub-standard.'

**279.** 'When I was first starting in this business I was advised to make sure that my name was always the largest in lights outside the theatre – that way people knew it was a show to avoid.'

**280.** 'Now we have a six-piece band – they only know six pieces.'

**281.** 'Our next stripper is so awful, if she was a building she'd be condemned.'

**282.** 'The last time this singer was here he gave a very moving performance. Everyone moved out of the theatre.'

**283.** 'If my parents knew I was here tonight as compère they'd be ashamed – they think I'm in prison.'

**284.** 'Now we have someone whom success hasn't changed at all – he's still the rotten, horrible person he always was.'

**285.** 'Now we have a great puppeteer who broke into the business by pulling a few strings.'

**286.** 'This is the last time I work as a compère at this club. My dressing room is so small every time I stand up I hit my head on the chain.'

**287.** Compère to heckler: Why don't you go and take a long walk off a short pier?

**288.** 'Our next singer once insured his voice for a million dollars. I wonder what he did with the money?'

**289.** 'We close the show tonight with Samson – who is sure to bring the house down.'

**290.** 'Now we have a rather portly trombonist. He could have been a violinist instead, if only he had known which chin to stick it under.'

# CONVERSATIONS

**291.** The best opener for any conversation is a bottle opener.

**292.** 'Of course I can keep secrets – it's the people I tell them to who can't.'

**293.** 'I bet I can make you talk like a Red Indian.'
'How?'
'There you are! I told you I could do it.'

**294.** I always know if it's a wrong number when my wife answers the phone – the conversation only lasts for twenty minutes.

**295.** My wife loves bitchy gossip – so does her best friend. Whenever they use the phone they speak poison to poison.

**296.** 'Clarissa is a thief, a liar and a murderer.'
'Oh – she must have improved since we were at school together.'

**297.** 'He's so unmusical he doesn't even know his brass from his oboe.'

**298.** 'I think she's got the makings of a star – already her head comes to a sharp point.'

**299.** Overheard at the blood donor clinic, 'I've come to donate a pint of blood – where do I spit it out?'

**300.** One response to people who like to ask, 'Is it cold out?' is to ask *them*, 'Is *what* cold out?'

**301.** Part of a phone conversation, 'Are you hanging up?'
'No, I'm lying down.'

**302.** 'Excuse me, do you know how to pronounce "Hawaii?" Is it with a "v" sound or a "w"?
'It's Havaii.'
'Thank you.'
'You're velcome.'

**303.** 'Are you trying to make a fool out of me?'
'Of course not! Why should I try to change Nature.'

**304.** 'Do you have holes in your trousers?'
'No.'
'Then how do you get your legs through?'

**305.** 'Are you a mechanic?'
'No. I'm a MacDonald.'


**306.** 'You've never looked better in your life . . . whenever *that* was.'


**307.** 'I'm trying.'
'Yes. You're *very* trying.'


**308:** Shaun: What's in your bag?

George: Chickens.

Shaun: Will you give me one of them?

George: No.

Shaun: If I guess how many you've got in your bag, then will you give me one?

George: Certainly! If you guess correctly, I'll give you both.

Sean: Six!


**309.** Mother: If you smartened yourself up you could get a job.

Son: Why?

Mother: Because in a job you get paid.

Son: So?

Mother: So then you can save some money.

Son: What for?

Mother: If you save enough you can eventually retire and not work any more.

Son: But I'm not working now.

**310.** 'I'm definitely *not* superstitious. It's bad luck to be superstitious.'

# DEFINITIONS

**311.** Aperitif: a pair of French false teeth.

**312.** Apricots: beds for baby apes.

**313.** Assets: baby donkeys.

**314.** Booby trap: a bra that is too small and too tight.

**315.** Derange: de place where de cowboys ride home to.

**316.** Disgruntled: a pig that has lost its voice.

**317.** Impale: to put in a bucket.

**318.** Inkling: a small bottle of ink.

**319.** Minister of Defence: a man who is always ready to lay down *your* life for *his* country.

**320.** Operator: a person who hates opera.

**321.** Pigtail: a story about a pig.

**322.** Politics: sounds coming from a parrot that has swallowed a watch.

**323.** Polygon: a dead parrot.

**324.** Polymath: a parrot that likes mathematics.

**325.** Triplets: small journeys.

# DOCTORS, DENTISTS & HEALTH

**326.** Last night my friend Mabel was feeling terribly ill so her husband phoned the doctor's surgery.

'I'm afraid the doctor is busy until 10 am Thursday,' said the receptionist.

'But that's three days away! My wife is terribly ill,' pleaded Mabel's husband. 'What if she's dead by then?'

'Well,' replied the receptionist, 'you can always phone and cancel the appointment.'

**327.** When Richard reached 50 he found that he always felt tired in the morning and afternoon, so he went to the doctor for advice.

After a physical examination and answering all the doctor's questions, the doctor said, 'You've been over-exerting yourself sexually. You say you have sex at least twice every night. I suggest you give up sex one night a week – say, on Wednesdays.'

'Oh,' said Richard, 'I couldn't give up sex on Wednesdays – that's the night I do it with my wife.'

**328.** A woman phoned her doctor and said, 'Doctor, you've got to help me. My husband thinks he's a refrigerator.'

The doctor told her not to worry. He was rather busy dealing with a flu epidemic and suggested that as her husband didn't appear to be harming anyone, he would come out and see him in a few days' time.

'But doctor,' said the woman. 'Can't you do anything *now*? He keeps opening and closing his mouth in his sleep – and the little light coming on and going off keeps waking me up.'

**329.** Last year I got ill. Since then I've been making payments on a Mercedes, a yacht and a villa in Spain – my doctors bought them.

**330.** Sally went to the doctor for an examination. 'You're pregnant,' said the doctor.

'Oh!' said Sally. 'Are you sure the baby is mine?'

**331.** When he went to the doctor and said he thought he was suffering from amnesia, the doctor asked him to pay in advance.

**332.** When he asked a doctor: 'Can you give me something for my head?' the doctor looked at him and said, '*Give* you something for it? I wouldn't even take it if you gave it to me for free.'

**333.** The young doctor had just been on a course on how to handle patients in a friendly and non-demeaning manner. Even if someone came to see him smelling like a sewer he was expected not to show his emotions or refer to a foul stench but should try to let the patient make the first reference to the smell. At all times, he should try to put patients at ease. A few days after the course, a huge lady knocked on the door to his surgery. He was delighted when she began the conversation by saying, 'Doctor, I think I'm a bit overweight.'

'That's OK,' soothed the doctor, remembering his training, 'just pull up three chairs and let's talk about it.'

**334.** The new doctor was making his round of the maternity ward and the first five women he saw were all expecting their babies on the same day: 28th March.

The doctor moved on to look at the sixth patient.

'And when is your baby expected?' asked the doctor.

'I don't know,' replied the woman, 'I didn't go to the office party like the other women in here did.'

**335.** Mrs Grunge: Doctor, it's about this bananas-only diet you've put me on.

Doctor: What about it?

Mrs Grunge: It seems to be having rather a peculiar effect on me.

Doctor: Oh, I wouldn't say that, Mrs Grunge. Now if you'll just stop scratching and come down from the curtains perhaps ...

**336.** Worried young girl: Doctor, this new diet you've put me on makes me feel so passionate and sexy that I got carried away last night and bit off my boyfriend's right ear.

Doctor: Don't worry, it's only about 40 to 50 calories.

**337.** I tried to follow my doctor's advice and give up smoking cigarettes and try chewing gum instead – but the matches kept getting stuck and the gum wouldn't light.

**338.** 'Doctor, doctor! How can I get this ugly mole off my face?'

'Get your dog to chase it back into its hole.'

**339.** Before I went off to India for my summer holidays I asked my doctor how I could avoid getting a disease from biting insects. He just told me not to bite any.

**340.** Handsome young doctor: Say 'ah!'

Pretty young girl: That's a change! Most young men want me to say 'yes'.

**341.** One of the patients in the hospital was petrified about having an operation.

'Don't worry,' soothed a nurse. 'Your surgeon is one of the best in his field. He's performed thousands of operations – and hasn't cut himself once.'

**342.** As the doctor said to his girlfriend, 'I love you with all my heart – and my kidneys, liver, epiglottis, spinal cord ...'

**343.** 'Doctor, doctor! I keep thinking I'm a pair of curtains.'

'Well, pull yourself together.'


**344.** When I asked my doctor to give me something to sharpen my appetite, he just gave me a razor blade.


**345.** Henry's doctor told him to be like a rabbit and eat lots of carrots to improve his eyesight, so he could see better at night in his work as a night watchman. His eyesight improved slightly, but he kept tripping over his ears.


**346.** Mrs Smith: Doctor, please can you help me? I've had twelve children and I'm pregnant again and I don't want any more kids after this one. I desperately need a hearing aid.

Doctor: A hearing aid? What do you want a hearing aid for? Surely you want some birth control pills or some form of contraceptive device?

Mrs Smith: No, doctor, I definitely want a hearing aid. You see, my husband gets drunk every Friday night and comes lumbering into my bed and says to me, 'Do you want to go to sleep or what?' Me being a bit deaf I always say, 'What?'


**347.** 'Doctor, is there something wrong with my heart?'

'I've given you a thorough examination and I can confidently say that your heart will last as long as you live.'

**348.** Doctor: Well, Mrs Cuthbert, I haven't seen you for a long time.

Mrs Cuthbert: I know, doctor. But I've been ill.


**349.** 'Doctor, doctor! My small son has just swallowed a roll of film.'
'Don't worry. Let him rest a bit and we'll wait and see what develops.'


**350.** Since I had treatment by a private doctor I've lost five kilos of weight. The doctor's bill was so enormous I've been unable to afford to buy any food to eat.


**351.** Last Tuesday I was in the doctor's waiting room and a young man came in with an expensive watch for the doctor.
'Thank you, thank you, thank you!' said the man, giving the doctor the expensive watch. 'This is a small token of my thanks for all your excellent treatment of my uncle.'
'But he died last week,' said the doctor.
'I know,' replied the young man. 'Thanks to your treatment I've just inherited five million pounds.'


**352.** 'Doctor, doctor, I was playing my mouth-organ and I suddenly swallowed it.'
'Well, look on the bright side – you could have been playing a grand piano.'

**353.** When I told the doctor's receptionist that I kept thinking I was a billiard ball, she told me to get to the end of the cue.

**354.** Yesterday I was in the doctor's waiting room and I heard a 96-year-old man pleading with the doctor for a lower sex drive.

'Surely you're imagining things,' said the doctor. 'You're 96 years old. Isn't all the feeling for sex just in your head?'

'Yes,' replied the elderly man, 'that's why I want you to lower my sex drive to the place where it might do more good.'

**355.** Patient: Doctor, doctor! I've just swallowed a whole sheep.

Doctor: How do you feel?

Patient: Quite baa-d.

**356.** The woman went to see the doctor. She had a large flower growing out of the top of her head.

The doctor looked at the flower and said, 'That is quite remarkable. I've never seen anything like that before. But I'll soon cut it off.'

'Cut it off?' snapped the woman. 'I don't want the flower cut off. I just want it treated against greenfly.'

**357.** While I was in the doctor's waiting room there was this tiny man only about six inches tall. Although he was there before me, he let me see the doctor first. I suppose he just had to be a little patient.

**358.** 'Doctor, doctor! Can you help me? My tongue keeps sticking out.'

'That's good. Now, if you can just lick these stamps …'


**359.** I went to the doctor this morning and told him I felt run down.

'Why do you feel that?' he asked.

'Because,' I replied, 'I've got tyre marks on my legs.'


**360.** Patient: Doctor, every time I eat fruit I get this strange urge to give people all my money.

Doctor: Would you like an apple or a banana?


**361.** When the doctor came to visit my Aunt Claudette, my aunt said, 'Doctor, I hope you're going to tell me that I'm very ill.'

The doctor looked at my aunt and said, 'But why? Don't you want me to say you're very healthy?'

'No,' replied Aunt Claudette. 'I feel absolutely terrible. And I don't want to feel like this if I'm healthy. But I'm sure you can make me better.'


**362.** Patient: Doctor, I've got diarrhoea.

Doctor: Yes. It runs in your family.


**363.** Doctor: Take three teaspoonfuls of this medicine after each meal.

Patient: But I've only got two teaspoons.

**364.** Patient: Doctor, I keep thinking I'm a ball of string.

Doctor: Well, go and get knotted.


**365.** Patient: Doctor, I've got wind – can you give me anything for it?

Doctor: How about a kite?


**366.** Old man: Doctor, how do I stand?

Doctor: That's what puzzles me.


**367.** Two doctors in the USA were talking.

First doctor: Why did you perform that operation on Mrs Weitzman?

Second doctor: Twenty thousand dollars.

First doctor: No. Perhaps you didn't hear me correctly. What did Mrs Weitzman have?

Second doctor: Twenty thousand dollars.


**368.** Frederick's wife was a surgeon, and so when Frederick had to go into hospital for an operation, she insisted on doing the surgery. She said that she didn't want anyone else to open her male.

**369.** Bernard was walking along the street one day when a young man rushed up to him and said, 'Can you show me the quickest way to get to the hospital?'

So Bernard pushed the young man under a bus.

**370.** There I was, lying ill in hospital, and my husband came into the room to read to me – my insurance policies and last will and testament.

**371.** A friend of mine recently went into hospital for an organ transplant. Now his body can play all the hymns in the church.

**372.** Hospital consultant: The woman in that bed is the love of my life.

Matron: Then why haven't you married her?

Hospital consultant: I can't afford to – she's a private patient.

**373.** The young woman was visiting the male psychiatrist for the first time, and he decided to test her reactions to different pictures.

First, he held up a card on which had been drawn two circles that almost touched.

'What does this make you think of?' asked the psychiatrist.

'Two fat people about to make love,' replied the young woman.

The psychiatrist showed the woman a picture of two wavy lines.

'That looks like the sand on the beach after two people have made passionate love for hours – or maybe it's a waterbed rocking in motion to some lovers in action.'

'Hmm,' said the psychiatrist, leaning back in his chair. 'You seem to be overly pre-occupied with sex.'

'How dare you!' snapped the woman. 'It was *you* that showed me the sexy pictures.'

**374.** One of the medical students has a lot of studying to do. He still thinks that varicose veins are veins that are too close together.

**375.** As he wandered along the hospital corridors he suddenly heard a man say, 'We'll tak a cup o'kindness yet, for auld lang syne.'

He walked towards the voice and entered a large room where a woman said:

'Gin a body meet a body
Coming through the rye;
Gin a body kiss a body,
Need a body cry?'

As a student of literature, he realised he was now in the Burns Unit.

**376.** I'm quite pleased with myself. I now only smoke three packets of cigarettes a day. I gave up cigarettes completely – I just smoke the packets.

**377.** Medical operations generally only take a few hours to perform – but the patients can spend very much longer boringly describing them to acquaintances.

**378.** The difference between a vitamin and a hormone is that you cannot hear a vitamin.

**379.** To make teenagers more comfortable when talking to him on his couch, a psychiatrist I know gives them a mobile phone to hold.

**380.** When my wife had a bad cold her young nephew recommended her to have a-choo-puncture.

**381.** A very posh lady lived in a large house in a small village. When several of her teeth began to ache she went to the dentist who explained the treatment she needed and said he was going to give her a local anaesthetic.

In plummy tones, the posh lady said, 'What? A *local* anaesthetic. But I'm a private patient. Give me one from London.'

**382.** The patient was complaining to his dentist about the cost of removing a bad tooth: 'You charge a lot of money for what will probably only take you a few minutes.'

'Well,' said the dentist, 'if you like I can pull the tooth very, very slowly and take an hour.'

**383.** The man was ushered into a chair by the dental assistant who told the dentist: 'This is Mr Bacon.'

The dentist looked at Mr Bacon and said: 'Lean back, please.'

# DRINKS & PUBS

**384.** Two drunks, Fred and Bill, were walking along the road when Fred said, 'Hey! Ishn't that man over th-there the Archbishop of Canterbury?'

'No,' replied Bill. 'It can't be.'

'It ish!' said Fred. 'I'll go over and ask him.'

Fred staggered over to the man and said, 'Ex ... excuse me. But are you the ... the Archbishop of Canterbury?'

'Get lost, you pathetic drunken creep,' replied the man, 'or I'll smash your face in!'

Fred staggered back to Bill.

'Was it the Archbish?' asked Bill.

'I don't know,' replied Fred. 'The st ... stupid man refushed to answer my question.'

**385.** An Irishman, a Scotsman, a priest, a rabbi, a feminist, an elephant and a duck walked into a bar and the barman said: 'Is this some kind of joke?'

**386.** A hamburger went into a bar and asked for a vodka. The barman looked at the hamburger and said: 'I'm sorry, but we don't serve food in here.'

**387.** Why do ugly women get picked up in bars by drunk men? Because beauty is in the eyes of the beer holder.

**388.** I was sitting in a bar when a man came in with an ostrich. As the ostrich lovingly nuzzled the man with its beak, the barmaid asked, 'Where did you get that creature?'

The man replied, 'I found an old bottle in the attic last night. When I opened the bottle a genie popped out and asked me to make a wish. I asked for a bird with long legs who'd love me.'

**389.** I asked my wife to give me a stiff drink and she put starch in my tea.

**390.** A large man with an enormous beer belly went into his usual pub, asked for a pint of beer, and then took a mirror out of his pocket.

'What are you going to do with the mirror?' asked the barmaid, as the man propped the mirror up on the bar counter.

'Look in it,' replied the man, sipping his pint of beer. 'My doctor told me today that I have to watch my drinking.'

**391.** At the bar last night was a man who demanded to be served a drink called Less.

'I've never heard of it,' said the barmaid.

'But you *must* have,' insisted the man.

'We don't have it. Is Less a new foreign beer or something?'

'I don't exactly know what it is,' replied the man, 'but my doctor insists that I should drink Less.'

**392.** The drunk was staggering along the street when he was stopped by the policeman.

'Excuse me, sir,' said the policeman, 'but where are you going?'

'I'm going to a lec . . . lecture,' replied the drunk.

'Who is giving the lecture?' asked the policeman.

'Wh . . . when I . . . when I g . . . get home,' said the drunk, 'my wife will give me the lecture.'

**393.** Brian's friend wanted to go to a topless bar – so Brian took him to a bar with no roof.

# ENTERTAINMENTS

**394.** Her husband awoke from a deep sleep and said to her: 'Please turn off the TV and let's have a drink and go to bed.'

She replied: 'I'm sorry, dear, that's not possible. We're still at the opera house.'

**395.** The artist was amazed that his first exhibition at a major gallery had been a sell-out.

'It's wonderful,' said the artist to the gallery owner.

'What sort of people bought my work?'

'Well,' said the gallery owner, 'initially, business was very slow and in the first week we only sold one picture – and that was to a man who tends to buy the cheapest painting in almost every exhibition we put on. He trusts our judgment and thinks the Art will prove to be a good long-term investment. Then a man came in and asked if you were prolific.'

'Did you tell him it takes me a long time to create each painting?' asked the artist.

'Yes,' replied the gallery owner. 'I said that what was on display was probably all the work you had completed for sale, and that there were only 50 to 100 other works which you had already sold or given away. He then asked if it was true that if an artist dies the value of his work increases. I said that quite often happens. He then pulled out his credit card and bought all your unsold work.'

'That's great!' said the artist. 'Who was he?'

The gallery owner replied: 'Your doctor.'

**396.** The ratings of a TV late-night current affairs interview series had plummeted. There were calls from the press and certain people within the TV organisation to cancel the show.

The researchers, producers, directors and presenters were naturally worried they might soon be made redundant and held a meeting to discuss the reasons for the fall in ratings and what could be done to improve the show.

'Viewers have gone off the main presenters,' said a brave researcher. 'Whereas one of the presenters used to be just mildly pompous – now many viewers think that he is also arrogant and condescending and just switch off.'

'Nonsense!' snapped a presenter. 'The problem is the quality of research. I'm frequently given notes that are wrong. What I want are clear signs of whether or not someone I'm interviewing is lying – then, if I've got firm proof, I can really attack him and call him a liar to his face.'

'I think I can help,' said a technician. 'My father is an award-winning scientist and he has been studying human behaviour for years. I'm sure that, for an appropriate fee, he could invent something that could spot the signs that someone is lying and indicate that to the interviewer.'

The senior producer thought the technician's idea was a good one and so the scientist was contracted to create a suitable lie detector.

After several weeks of feverish activity, the scientist produced a chair that looked exactly like all the other chairs used by people being interviewed on the show. But hidden inside the chair were complicated monitoring systems that checked changes in the body temperature, sweat rate, pulse, tenseness, changes in tone of voice and a whole host of other factors that would indicate whether or not someone sitting in the chair was giving a lying answer to a question.

To indicate to the presenter the severity of the lie, the chair would give the person being interviewed a very mild electric shock. The person would then give a slight, almost unnoticeable twitch for which the presenter should be alert. The worse the lie, the greater the shock – which would have the added advantage of causing the interviewee to feel somewhat uncomfortable so he or she might then start to make obvious mistakes. The shocks might even provoke lying interviewees into fits of anger – which would be especially good for the ratings. No one would suspect that the chair was responsible for the shocks.

Everyone was delighted with the chair. One of the presenters was chosen to test it. When he was sitting comfortably he was asked: 'What is the capital of England?' When he replied, 'Edinburgh', he gave a small twitch.

Watching a replay of the tape of his questioning, the presenter said the shock was so mild he had not been conscious of the twitch it provoked.

The production team were ecstatic. They decided to put the chair into use on that evening's show when a prominent politician was due to be interviewed about the Government's policies.

Thus it was that the repeat screenings of that interview attracted record ratings all around the world. The interviewer asked the politician an opening easy question and the politician began: 'I think ...' – and the chair and the politician exploded in a burst of sparks and flames.

**397.** A friend of mine once went to a naughty cabaret show where the stripper was so ugly that, when she was halfway through her act, the audience shouted, 'Put them on! Put them on!'

**398.** I've given up trying to see a film at the cinema. Last night I bought five separate tickets and *still* I didn't get in to see the film.

Every time I bought a ticket and went towards the film theatre a stupid man took my ticket and tore it in half – so I had to get another one. Then he would do the same to that one, too.

**399.** When I go to the cinema, I want to be entertained. I want to see adventure stories and comedies. I *don't* want to see sex, violence and bad language – I get all that from my wife.

**400.** Cloakroom attendant: Please leave your hat here, sir.

Club customer: I don't have a hat.

Cloakroom attendant: Then I'm sorry, sir, but you cannot come into the Club. I have orders that people cannot enter unless they leave their hat in the cloakroom.

**401.** When the nightclub singer asked me if he sang in the right key, I said he sang more like a monkey.

**402.** I refused to watch the new TV series about the life and times of Ethelred the Unready. It should not have been screened – there's too much Saxon violence.

**403.** Costumes designed by Plaster of Paris.

**404.** Tents supplied by Marquee de Sade.

**405.** Comedian: Laughter is a wonderful thing – so other comics tell me!

**406.** People say that with all the developments in television – cable, satellite, digital, high definition – that TV will eventually completely replace newspapers. But have you ever tried to swat a fly with a television set?

# FAMILIES

**407.** The young boy came home from school and asked his father, 'Dad, is it true that I am a descendant of apes?'

'I'm not really sure,' replied the father. 'I don't know much about your mother's side of the family.'

**408.** A friend of mine looked really worried. 'Is there anything wrong?' I asked.

'I'm going to be a father,' he replied.

'Then why are you looking so gloomy?' I asked. 'Surely it's a happy occasion. Isn't your wife pleased at having a baby?'

My friend sighed and said: 'It's not hers.'

**409.** The most reliable method of determining a baby's sex is childbirth.

**410.** Despite advances in medical science he believes old women should not have babies. He thinks they might do to babies what they do with car keys and spectacles: put them down somewhere and forget where they left them.

**411.** Every Sunday afternoon I visit my parents. Then all my brothers and sisters arrive and we do some charity work – making jerseys. We're a very close knit family.

**412.** When I was a small boy my family were so poor we could only afford alphabet soup with two letters in it.

**413.** When I was a small boy my parents used to give me pocket money and showed me a large money box to put it in. Whenever I got given money from relatives for Christmas and birthdays, my parents encouraged me to put it in that box. It was only when I was about 10 years old that I discovered the large money box was the electricity meter.

**414.** When I was a small boy my father took me into the woods to go hunting – he only gave me a 10 second start ...

**415.** When Jeremy was a child he realised he was unloved when he was kidnapped. When the kidnappers sent his parents a ransom note his father replied asking for proof that they really did hold his son. The kidnappers cut off one of Jeremy's fingers and sent it to his father. His mother then asked the kidnappers to provide more proof.

**416.** He realised how much his family cared about him when he ran away from home. No one in his family was able to give the police his description.

**417.** When he asked to be buried at sea, his family hired a team of divers to dig his grave.

**418.** A man is seriously ill in hospital and his wife and five children visit him. They tell him how much they love him and, after wishing him well with his operation, the children leave the ward so he can talk privately with their mother.

'Darling,' said the man, 'you and the children all think I'm having an operation. But the surgeon told me today my condition has got worse. There are too many complications and I may not survive the night.'

The man's wife burst into tears as he continued: 'There is one thing I've always been unsure of and I hope you will answer honestly. All our children have dark hair, like you and me, except for the youngest, who has light brown hair. I can understand if he's not mine and you had a brief affair. I forgive you. But is he mine?'

'Yes,' replied the wife. 'I can honestly tell you he really is your son.'

Her husband smiled and lapsed into unconsciousness. His wife softly muttered to herself: 'Thank goodness he didn't ask me about the other four ...'

**419.** His brother is a man of rare gifts – he rarely gives any.

**420.** When I told my children that I used to be young once, they congratulated me on having such a long memory.

**421.** Clive was in a bar, having a quiet drink with some of his friends. Suddenly, a man lurched into the bar, looked at Clive and shouted: 'I've just had sex with your mother!' Then he ran out of the bar.

Clive blushed and his friends tried hard not to smirk. They continued their drinking for another hour or so until the same man came back into the bar and shouted at Clive: 'We've done it again! She may be old, with droopy boobs, but she's still got stamina. Sex with your mother was fantastic!'

One of Clive's friends whispered to Clive, 'If you want, I'll help you take him outside and give him a beating. What he's shouting is disgusting!'

Clive, embarrassed, said to the man who had shouted at him: 'Please leave me alone. I know it's very rare for you to have sex – but there's no need to shout about it. I'll meet you outside and we can talk quietly about it when I've finished my drink, Dad.'


**422.** The house-proud woman gave birth to twins. She kept her house immaculately clean. The kitchen permanently smelt of disinfectant.

The twin's milk bottles were always thoroughly sterilized; their clothes washed in the most powerful of washing powders to remove any germs.

Then, when the twins started to get a bit grumpy and grizzly, she asked a friend who had successfully coped with triplets what she should do.

'Oh,' said the friend, 'the twins are probably just teething. Why don't you put your finger in their mouths and . . .'

'What!' shrieked the twins' mother. 'Don't you have to boil the finger first?'


**423.** The reason they call the TV control a 'remote' is that with a sports-mad husband in the house and five teenage children a wife has a remote chance of controlling the channel.


**424.** My uncle in Canada told me that he would leave me a large sum in his will. Last month he passed away and the lawyer read the will. The large sum was: 1.5

million multiplied by 358.5 divided by 52.5 minus 10,242,852. (The sum was large – but when I went to collect the money I found the amount was small – only around $5.)

**425.** When I was a child, my family were so poor that the only thing I got on my birthday was a year older.

**426.** When the Mexican fireman had twin sons he had them christened Jose and Hose B.

**427.** I once knew a couple who wanted their baby to behave during its christening and so they practised every day for a week before the service by using the kitchen sink.

**428.** I've stopped living in a house. I now live in a kennel. My kids made all my books dog-eared, my wife treats me like a dog, and all my work makes me dog-tired – so I might as well stay in the kennel.

**429.** I think my three young sons are going to be plumbers when they grow up – they never come when they're called.

**430.** The quickest way to find long-lost relatives is for the news to leak out that you have won the Lottery.

**431.** He was lazing on the sofa, watching TV and drinking beer, when his wife told him to get up and take the children to the zoo. He took another sip of his beer, belched, and said to his wife, 'If the zoo wants the children, I'm sure they'll bring a cage and come and collect them.'

**432.** Mr Smith was always so busy working that he never had much time to spend with his son.

Then, on his son's 17th birthday, Mr Smith managed to get away from his office to take his son for a birthday lunch at an expensive restaurant.

'Cor!' said the son, when one of the waitresses took their coats. 'Look at the size of her boobs. I wonder what she's like in bed.'

Mr Smith was rather alarmed at his son's comments, but they were soon seated in the restaurant and father and son exchanged gossip and news.

Just as they were about to leave the restaurant, an attractive young woman entered.

'Wow!' exclaimed Mr Smith's son in a loud voice. 'Her boobs are fantastic. I really fancy her.'

Mr Smith was embarrassed. His son appeared to have turned into an uncouth, chauvinistic yob. Maybe the boy's school was to blame.

Thus it was that Mr Smith's son was removed from the local school and sent away to the upper form in one of Britain's most expensive public schools. It was surely not too late for the boy to learn some manners.

On his son's 18th birthday Mr Smith took his son to the same restaurant as before – and Mr Smith was delighted at the way his son behaved. He was polite, well-mannered and did not make uncouth remarks about the waitresses but treated them with charm and was a perfect gentleman.

The son talked of his plans for university, and Mr Smith was just about to comment on the amazing transformation of his son into a man with excellent behaviour – surely the work of the public school – when the son looked at one of the waiters and said, 'Look at that! Isn't that a cute bottom? I wonder what he's like in bed.'

**433.** My teenage son is always borrowing money from me to entertain his girlfriends. Yesterday evening I answered the phone and a young woman asked: 'Is that dreamboat?'

'No,' I replied, 'it's supply ship.'

**434**. Every family should have two children. That way, if one of them becomes a poet or a painter, the other can give them financial support.

**435.** My sister was asked if she'd like to be a baby sitter – but she said she thought it cruel to sit on babies.

**436.** My sister has visited another planet. This morning she trod on a chocolate bar and said she'd just set foot on Mars.

**437.** My sister isn't really fat – but when her boyfriend filled her shoe with champagne it took five bottles to do it.

**438.** I wouldn't say my sister was an ugly baby – but it was almost a year before my mother realized she had been putting the nappy on the wrong end.

**439.** When my brother was a small boy he once slept with his head under the pillow. When he woke up he found 28 £1 coins – and all his teeth were missing: the fairies had taken them.

**440.** I wouldn't say my sister is desperate for a boy-friend, but when she went to the station and asked for a ticket from Bournemouth to London, the young male ticket clerk asked, 'Single?' – and she replied, 'Yes. Are you are asking for a date?'

**441.** When I was a small boy, my mother used to give me vitamins B1, B2, B6, B12 and B quiet.

# FOOD & RESTAURANTS

**442.** Her doctor told her she should stop having intimate dinners for four – unless there were three other people with her.

**443.** She said she couldn't possibly go on a celebrity diet. She didn't want to eat famous people.

**444.** I know a woman who went on what is called the 'Hollywood Actress Diet' – three males a day.

**445.** The secret of successful dieting is said to be the triumph of mind over platter.

**446.** I went to a restaurant the other day and when the waiter brought me the menu I asked him, 'What do you recommend?'
He said, 'The restaurant just around the corner.'

**447.** I was in a restaurant recently and I overheard a man ask the waiter, 'How do you prepare the chicken?'
The waiter replied, 'Well, we sit the chicken down calmly, give it a sip of whisky and then say to it: "I'm sorry, but you're going to have to die".'

**448.** When the waiter came towards me carrying my meal I noticed he was pressing two of his fingers down on to my fish.

'Excuse me,' I said to the waiter. 'It's not very hygienic putting your fingers on my food.'

'Well,' said the waiter, 'it's better than the fish falling off the plate on to the floor again.'

**449.** When he went to a restaurant and saw that it displayed a notice, 'Ties Must Be Worn', he thought he would be refused admission as his tie was brand new and not worn.

**450.** A gay couple were celebrating their tenth anniversary together by having a romantic meal in an expensive restaurant. However, the atmosphere was rather spoilt by a man and a woman at the next table having a fierce argument.

'See,' said one of the gay men, 'I told you mixed marriages can have problems.'

**451.** The male students at the university consider a balanced diet to be a beer in one hand and a pie in the other hand.

**452.** University students believe there are three main food groups – frozen, canned and take-away.

**453.** When I was asked how my stomach grew so large, I said it must have just *snacked* up on me.

**454.** She realised she was rather fat when she gave one of her dresses to a charity shop and a group of scouts bought it to use as a tent.

**455.** My husband is so fat they refused to let him go bungee jumping off the local bridge – they thought he might make it collapse.

**456.** The best way to lose weight is not to exceed the feed limit.

**457.** If swimming is supposed to be a good way of losing weight – then why are whales so huge?

**458.** When I went on a diet of baked beans and garlic, all I lost was ten friends.

**459.** The only things his wife knows how to make for dinner are restaurant reservations.

**460.** My girlfriend makes melt-in-your-mouth dinners. She always forgets to defrost them.

**461.** My husband's cooking is so bad that when he cooks for a dinner party the guests pray before the meal – and after it.

**462.** My wife's cakes are so stodgy and heavy that when I throw them out for the birds to eat, the birds then have to *walk* South for the winter.

**463.** When his wife read the recipe instructions to separate two eggs, she kept one in the kitchen and put one in the lounge.

**464.** Rhubarb always seems to look like rather embarrassed celery.

**465.** 'I still feel rather sick,' said Barbara to her best friend.

'Do you know what caused it?' asked the friend.

'I think it must have been the oysters I ate last night,' said Barbara.

'Were they bad?' asked the friend. 'What did they look like when you opened them?'

'Oh!' said Barbara. 'You mean you're supposed to *open* them before you eat them.'

**466.** I once saw a man eat a pocket watch. Then he swallowed two wristwatches. He said I could stay and see him swallow even more watches – but I said I thought it was very time-consuming.

**467.** 'I'm going to eat a pet,' said the small girl to her brother.

'You can't do that!' protested the brother. 'It's cruel and they will taste horrible.'

'I *am* going to eat a pet,' insisted the sister, defiantly.

The boy was almost in tears as he asked his sister, 'Is it the kitten or the puppy you're going to eat?'

'Neither,' replied the sister. 'The pet I'm going to eat is a crumpet!'


**468.** A miserly couple went to a restaurant in London and each of them ordered a steak.

The waiter was surprised to see the woman eating while the man merely looked at his plate without eating.

'Is there something wrong with your meal, sir?' asked the waiter.

'Oh, no!' replied the man. 'It's just that my wife is using the dentures first.'


**469.** I was once invited by a business colleague for a meal in an expensive restaurant while on a sales trip to Germany.

The whole restaurant was decorated with the stuffed heads of animals. We had to sit next to a wall on which was hung the huge head of a rhinoceros.

'My goodness!' I said to the waiter. 'That rhino looks fierce.'

'It was,' admitted the waiter. 'It killed my father.'

'I'm sorry to hear that,' I said. 'Did it happen on safari in Africa?'

'No,' said the waiter. 'It happened here in Germany. My father was sitting in a chair underneath the rhino head when it dropped off the wall and hit him.'

**470.** Times were hard. Keith was sacked from his office job and went to work as a waiter in a restaurant. Soon after, one of his fellow redundant office workers came in.

'Fancy seeing *you* working in a place like *this*,' scoffed the man.

'So?' replied Keith. 'Fancy *you* being reduced to having to eat in a dump like this!'

**471.** David: I know this lovely little restaurant where we can eat dirt cheap.

Barbara: Cheap or not, I don't fancy eating dirt.

**472.** When the waiter asked my boyfriend if he wanted a fingerbowl, he replied, 'No thank you, I don't eat fingers.'

**473.** My hotel is quite nice. At dinner in the restaurant last night there was a young girl at a table next to mine. She had chicken breasts and frog's legs – but her face was beautiful.

**474.** Man: Can I have a table for dinner?

Waiter: Certainly, sir. Do you want the table fried, boiled, steamed or roasted?

**475.** The cannibal looked down at his soup with distaste. He had asked his wife for a change from humans. Perhaps she would make monkey soup? But no, his wife had made the soup from a pilot who had crashed in the jungle.

'What,' asked the cannibal, 'is this flier doing in my soup?'

# GHOSTS

**476.** I recently went to see a boxing match between two ghosts – they fought at phantom weight.

**477.** I know a beautiful female ghost who used to have her photo on the front pages of glossy magazines. She was a cover ghoul.

**478.** I was woken in the night by strange crashing sounds coming from the kitchen. I crept downstairs and saw a strange apparition throwing crockery on the floor. It looked like the ghost of a giant chicken – it was a poultry-geist.

**479.** The father ghost told his son, 'Spook only when you are spoken to.'

**480.** Richard was not very frightened when he saw the ghost and, since it appeared to be friendly, he asked the ghost if he could try to photograph it.

The ghost willingly agreed and Richard went to fetch his camera, but found that the flash attachment on it was broken.

The spirit was willing – but the flash was weak.

**481.** Then there was the ghost who didn't believe in people.

**482.** Human: Do you plan to stay in this town very long?

Ghost: No – I'm only passing through.

**483.** The young ghost got very scared when his friends told him too many human stories.

**484.** It was a graveyard romance. Boy meets ghoul.

**485.** Some years ago I tried to become a ghost writer. But I couldn't find any ghosts who wanted me to write for them.

**486.** Where do ghosts take their dirty coats?
  To a dry-screamers.

**487.** What did the phantom on guard duty outside the haunted castle say when he heard a noise?
  'Halt! Who ghosts there?'

**488.** Why was the shy ghost frightened of going to the opticians' party?
  Because he thought he might make a spooktackle of himself.

**489.** What do you call a female ghost who serves drinks and food on a plane?
An air ghostess.


**490.** What music do ghosts like?
Haunting melodies.


**491.** How did the two ghosts fall in love?
It was love at first fright.


**492.** On what day do ghosts play tricks on each other?
April Ghoul's Day.


**493.** Where can you catch a ghost train?
At a manifestation.


**494.** Why did the female ghoul like demons?
Because demons are a ghoul's best friend.


**495.** What is the favourite ride of ghosts at a fairground?
The roller-ghoster.

# HOLIDAYS & HOTELS

**496.** A small boy was enjoying building a sandcastle with his father on the beach in Bournemouth.

'I'll get some water to fill the moat round the castle,' said the boy and took a plastic bucket and ran towards the sea. He found it great fun running in and out of the waves. Then he decided to collect some shells to decorate the castle.

After about fifteen minutes of wandering along the beach he suddenly realised he was lost. Fortunately, a lifeguard was nearby so the small boy went to him and said, 'Please can you help me? I've lost my Dad.'

The lifeguard looked at him reassuringly and asked, 'What's he like?'

'Beer and curries,' replied the boy.


**497.** Last summer I was trekking through a country in Africa when I came across a huge hippopotamus lying dead on the bank of a river. Somehow, the death did not look like natural causes. I turned to my guide and asked, 'Who killed the hippo?'

The guide shouted in a native language and a pygmy came out from behind a tree. 'Pygmy kill hippo,' said the guide.

'How can such a small person kill such a large creature?' I asked, and the guide translated my words to the pygmy and then translated his response: 'With a club.'

'It must have been a very large club,' I said.

'Yes,' replied the pygmy. 'There are over a hundred of us in it.'

**498.** The bellboy knocked on Claude's hotel room door.

'Your suitcases, sir,' said the bellboy, wheeling them into the room.

After he had arranged the suitcases, the bellboy asked:

'Is there anything else I can get you, sir?'

'No thanks,' said Claude, giving the bellboy a tip.

The bellboy heard sounds of water splashing in the bathroom and saw a lady's dress lying on the bed.

'Perhaps your wife might like something?' suggested the bellboy.

'Oh!' said Claude. 'I almost forgot. Can you get me a postcard to send to her?'


**499.** I recently stayed in such a cheap hotel that the staff stole towels from the guests.


**500.** My wife and I have recently returned from a luxury cruise. On our first day at sea we received a note from the captain asking us to sit with him at dinner.

We didn't join him as my wife thought it was outrageous that we should pay a small fortune to go on the cruise and then be expected to eat with the staff.


**501.** The young man was on his first ever holiday abroad. As he lay on the beach in a crowded part of Spain, a gorgeous young woman lay down beside him and kept making admiring glances at him.

Eventually, she said, 'I like the look of you. Would you like to come back to my apartment for a little game?'

'Fantastic!' replied the young man. 'I was just wondering where I'd find a snooker table.'

**502.** Last year on holiday we went to this strange place where there were lots of stalls with people hassling us to buy different types of jelly and custard – it was a trifle bazaar.

**503.** The Chinese girl had just returned to Singapore from a holiday in England and was talking to her best friend.

'Lynn, I've been thinking about Keith ever since I left England. Now I'm back home I don't think I should write to him as our friendship was only slight.'

'But, Sue, you promised to marry him!'

'I know. But that was all.'

**504.** Mother, in holiday apartment: Sarah, can you wash up the dishes?

Sarah: But we don't have any rubber gloves. You know that water isn't very good for my skin.

Mother: Is that why you've spent most of the day in the sea?

**505.** My hotel is so noisy I couldn't sleep at all last night.

I complained to the hotel manager and said I had specifically requested a quiet room. He said the *room* was quiet – it was the traffic outside, the lift next to it, and the people in all the other rooms that were noisy.

**506.** You can always tell if you're in a honeymoon hotel – all the couples start yawning at five in the afternoon.

**507.** 'Are the sheets clean?' asked a tourist at a small hotel in New York.

'Of course, they're clean,' snapped the manager. 'I washed them only yesterday. If you don't believe me, you can feel them – they're still damp.'

**508.** Hotel receptionist: Would you like a room with a private bath?

Young man: That's all right, I'm not shy. I don't mind who sees me. The bath doesn't *have* to be private.

**509.** My wife and I once stayed in an ancient hotel in an overseas resort. The corridors of the hotel had cobwebs and the swimming pool had green slime on it.

On the first morning of our stay we were woken by a pounding on the door.

I staggered out of bed, looked at my watch (it was 6 am) and opened the door.

'Sheets!' said a plump, middle-aged maid.

'What?' I asked.

'Sheets!' repeated the maid.

'We've got sheets,' I said. 'It's only six o'clock in the morning. Surely you don't change the sheets that early? We're staying in this hotel for another three days.'

'Sheets! Give me sheets,' insisted the maid, pushing past me and into the room, whereupon she started pulling the sheets off the bed.

'This is ridiculous,' said my wife. 'Can't you leave changing the sheets until later?'

'No time,' said the maid. 'Need sheets now for breakfast.'

'Why?' I asked.

'Must have sheets,' said the maid. 'Need to put on tables as tablecloths for breakfast.'

**510.** A man arrived at a hotel in a large conference town.

'Do you have a room for the night?' he asked.

'I'm sorry,' said the receptionist, 'but we are fully booked. All the other hotels are probably full, too.'

'But surely,' said the man, 'you must be able to find some room somewhere? Suppose I was the Prime Minister in disguise – surely you'd find a room for him?'

'Yes, we would,' admitted the receptionist.

'Well,' said the man, 'as the Prime Minister isn't coming, please can I have his room?'


**511.** I didn't have much trouble speaking Italian when I was on holiday in Italy – it was just that the Italians seemed to have trouble understanding it.


**512.** I was standing in a queue in a hamburger restaurant the other day when I overheard two girls talking. One girl was blonde, the other brunette.

'Did you manage to pick up any Italian when you were on holiday in Rome?' asked the blonde.

'Yes,' replied the brunette. 'Lots.'

'Let's hear some,' said the blonde.

'Well,' replied the brunette, 'they all spoke almost perfect English.'


**513.** There I was on the beach on the far-off paradise island when suddenly I was surrounded by a horde of shouting natives.

They moved in closer and closer and their shouts grew louder and their gestures grew more menacing and dramatic – so I had to give in and buy a cheap necklace and a gaudy T-shirt.

**514.** Our safari holiday was very disappointing. The weather was terrible and the only game we saw were the locals playing snooker.

**515.** Whenever I go to stay with people they always ask me how I slept. How do they think I slept! Do they think I'm odd or something? I sleep like everyone else – with my eyes closed.

**516.** You only get really terrible sunburn if you bask for it.

**517.** A comedian went on holiday to a remote island where he got lost in the jungle. He was captured by cannibals who cooked him for their evening meal. Soon after they started eating, one of the cannibals asked: 'Do you think this meat tastes a bit funny?'

# KNOCK KNOCK

**518.** 'Knock, knock.'

'Who's there?'

'Machiavelli.'

'Machiavelli who?'

'Machiavelli nice suit for £95.'


**519.** 'Knock, knock.'

'Who's there?'

'Luke.'

'Luke who?'

'Luke through the keyhole and you'll see who.'


**520.** 'Knock, knock.'

'Who's there?'

'Cook.'

'Cook who?'

'Oh, I didn't know it was Spring already.'

**521.** 'Knock, knock.'

'Who's there?'

'Ken.'

'Ken who?'

'Ken you please open the door and let me in.'

**522.** 'Knock, knock.'

'Who's there?'

'Hatch.'

'Hatch who?'

'Bless you!'

**523.** 'Knock, knock.'

'Who's there?'

'Who.'

'Who who?'

'Sorry, I don't talk to owls.'

**524.** 'Knock, knock.'

'Who's there?'

'Cows.'

'Cows who?'

'Cows don't go "who" they go "moo".'


**525.** 'Knock, knock.'

'Who's there?'

'Mary.'

'Mary who?

'Mary Christmas and a Happy New Year.'


**526.** 'Knock, knock.'

'Who's there?'

'Howard.'

'Howard who?'

'Howard you like to stand here in the freezing cold and snow while some twit keeps asking "Who"?

# LEGAL MATTERS

**527.** When she was asked why she had killed her husband by using a bow and arrow, she explained, 'I didn't want to make a noise and wake the kids.'

**528.** Mr and Mrs Jones were just coming out of the hotel car park when they saw their car being driven away.

'Stop thief!' shouted Mr Jones. As the car sped away, he turned to his wife and asked: 'Did you get a good look at the driver? Could you describe him to the police?'

'No,' replied Mrs Jones. 'But I did manage to remember the licence number of the car.'

**529.** Last night a man broke a fishmonger's window and stole all the crustaceans. It was a smash and *crab* raid.

**530.** Her mother was a shoplifter. Unfortunately, she took after her.

**531.** When she returned home from a party, Candy discovered that her house had been burgled. She quickly phoned the police and sat calmly until a police van arrived. As she went to open the front door, she saw a policeman with an Alsatian dog get out of the van. Candy burst into tears and sobbed: 'I've been burgled – and what do the police send? A blind cop with his guide dog.'

**532.** John had been in prison for only three months when he got into a fight with another prisoner who sliced off John's ear with a knife. A short time later he got tonsillitis and had his tonsils removed. Then John got a mouth infection and had to have six teeth extracted. Soon after that, his hand got slammed in a door and he had to have the tips of three fingers amputated.

A few weeks later John had appendicitis and his appendix was taken out. It was at this point that a prison warder went to the governor of the prison and warned: 'I think John is escaping bit by bit.'

**533.** When he arrived home looking tired and exhausted, the judge sighed and told his wife, 'It's been another trying day.'

**534.** The prosecution lawyer was questioning the defendant. 'You took money from friends, relatives and work colleagues telling them that you would invest it on their behalf. Yet instead of investing it, you used it to live the high life. How could you take money from people who trusted you?'

The defendant looked at the lawyer and said: 'Isn't it obvious? Who else would give me money? People who didn't trust me would be unlikely to give me any.'

**535.** What happened to the woman who was caught stealing a battery?

She was put in a dry cell.

**536.** He thought the judge was being lenient in giving him a suspended sentence – until he was taken out of the courtroom and led to the gallows.

**537.** Yesterday I was standing in a queue in a fast food restaurant when a man pointed a gun at a counter assistant and said, 'Give me all the money in your till.'

The counter assistant asked, 'Will that be to use here, or to take away?'

**538.** Late last night a large quantity of sand and cement were stolen from a builder's yard. Police are hunting for some concrete evidence.

**539.** When the burglars broke into his house they could see that his wife had left him. The house plants were all dead and the only sign of life was the stuff growing in the refrigerator.

**540.** Philip was sent to prison for making big money. He made it half a centimetre too big.

**541.** When the policeman caught Fred stealing a lady's undergarment from a washing line, Fred pleaded with the cop not to arrest him, saying, 'It was my first slip.'

**542.** He used to be a burglar – but it was his shortsightedness that got him caught. Late one night he climbed into a house through an open window. He could hear sounds of gentle snoring from people asleep in the bedrooms so he made his way silently to the lounge. He twiddled some knobs on what he thought was the safe – and the radio blared out loud music.

**543.** Lawyers believe that the best thing in life are fees.

**544.** Lawyers don't *give* bad advice – they *charge* for it.

**545.** Anyone who says talk is cheap hasn't employed a lawyer.

**546.** If there's a lawyer involved, then where there's a will there's a delay.

**547.** Sherlock Holmes was in his study reading a newspaper. Watson entered and Sherlock looked up and said, 'I believe that you were in a hurry early this morning.'

'Yes,' replied Watson. 'How did you know that?'

'And,' said Sherlock, 'I deduce that you are wearing your pink-striped underpants.'

'My goodness!' said Watson. 'How do you know that?'

'Because,' replied Sherlock, 'you have forgotten to put your trousers on.'

**548.** She was stopped by the police for speeding. The police claimed she was travelling at over 100 miles per hour. She denied the charge as she said she couldn't possibly have done that as she had only been driving for fifteen minutes.

**549.** The young woman was forced to stop her car by the police. 'Didn't you see the 30 miles an hour sign?' asked a policeman.

'No,' replied the woman. 'I was driving too fast to see it.'

**550.** When he was arrested in a foreign country he was pleased when he heard the chief of police tell him, 'You will get a fair trial' – but wept when the police chief continued: 'and then you will be shot.'

**551.** The detective had a good reputation for solving crimes – but this was because in all his cases people either left obvious clues or witnesses came forward to point out the criminals. That was why the detective's colleagues called him Sheer-Luck Holmes.

**552.** If it is the law of gravity that keeps us from falling off the Earth as it zooms around the Sun, what kept us on Earth before the law was passed?

**553.** 'Now,' said the prosecution counsel to the lady in the witness box, 'at the time of the car crash, what gear were you in?'

'Umm,' mused the lady, 'I think it was blue jeans and a tight white T-shirt.'

**554.** The complicated commercial lawsuit had dragged on for years and years.

'I've had enough of this,' said the managing director of one of the firms involved. 'Let's come to a compromise solution and settle out of court.'

'Impossible!' snorted the City solicitor. 'My firm is determined to fight your case right down to your last penny.'


**555.** 'Do you plead guilty or not guilty?'

'Don't I have any other choices?'


**556.** The solicitor died and went to the gates of Heaven where he was to be interviewed by St Peter to see if he should be let into Heaven or sent down to Hell.

'I don't know why I died so young,' said the solicitor. 'It doesn't seem fair. I'm only 35.'

'I know,' replied St Peter. 'But according to all the time you've billed your clients for, you're at least 208!'


**557.** The most difficult task a young lawyer ever had was the evening he spent trying to change a beautiful young lady's will.


**558.** Albert had just been found guilty of killing his very bossy and argumentative wife by pushing her out of the window of a room on the 29th floor of a hotel.

'This is a very serious offence,' said the judge. 'If your wife had fallen on someone, there could have been a very nasty accident.'

**559.** The defendant in one court case said that at the time the crime was committed he was in hospital recovering from a vicious attack by a shark while swimming in the sea: he therefore had a water-bite alibi.


**560.** 'Members of the jury, have you reached your verdict?'

'Yes we have, your honour. We find the gorgeously sexy woman who stole the jewellery not guilty.'


**561.** 'Thank you for winning the case,' said the grateful client to her solicitor. He had won her £35,000 from the local council as she had tripped over an uneven paving slab on the pavement and injured her leg.

'It was a pleasure,' said the solicitor, handing the client his bill.

The client took the bill, then frowned: 'This bill is pretty steep. Is it right?'

'Of course,' replied the solicitor. 'It represents good value for all our time, care, experience, expertise and legal knowledge. If it wasn't for us, you wouldn't have won the case.'

'But your costs are almost half the damages,' replied the client. 'If it wasn't for me, you wouldn't have had a case.'

'But,' said the solicitor, 'anyone can trip over a paving slab.'


**562.** The man had been arrested and charged with stealing 500 cigars.

He consulted a solicitor for advice and was quoted a fee for defending him.

'I can't afford all that!' exclaimed the man. 'I'm completely innocent. Wouldn't you like some boxes of cigars instead of a cash fee?'

**563.** Amanda Guv dyed her hair blonde when she became a policewoman so that when she made an arrest people could genuinely say, 'It's a fair cop, Guv.'

**564.** The police were rather suspicious when Bo Peep said she had lost her sheep. She had a crook with her.

**565.** Detective's assistant: Sir, I have found a box of vestas with your name on it.

Detective: Ah! So at last I have met my match.

**566.** We're continually hearing about the terrible crime rate in America, but is it true?

For example, when I arrived in New York a few months ago, a man sidled up to me and said, 'Want to buy a watch?'

'How much?' I asked.

'Sssh!' said the man, 'the guy next to you is still wearing it.'

**567.** I read in the newspaper today that a lot of people have recently been attacked at night and bitten just above the knee. Police are looking for a very short vampire.

# MARRIAGE

**568.** 'I'm terribly worried,' said the bride-to-be to her mother. 'There is so much to organise for the wedding. It could easily all go wrong. What if I forget an apparently insignificant item? It could still turn into a shambles.'

'Don't worry,' said her mother. 'I'll make absolutely sure the groom gets there.'

**569.** John got tired of his wife forever picking on him and being argumentative. He was therefore glad to divorce her. Unfortunately, when he slipped behind with his maintenance payments she repossessed him.

**570.** The middle-aged businessman returned from honeymoon with his young wife and showed her around his country house, telling her she could make whatever changes she liked: change the furniture, the wall coverings, and do a complete re-design of the entire house – whatever would make her happy.

A few days later the businessman had to return to his City office and apartment. His young wife soon set about making changes to the country house.

That weekend, when the businessman returned home, his wife embraced him and said she had prepared his dinner.

'I'll just get a bottle of wine from the cellar,' said the businessman. But when he entered the cellar he was shocked. Row after row of wine racks were completely empty. He could only find a few bottles of non-vintage wine.

'Darling,' called the businessman, 'where have you put the rest of the wine?'

'I had a major clear out,' replied his young wife. 'You had some really old bottles. Didn't you read the labels? It's not healthy to keep out-of-date stuff so I threw away all the wine that was past the date written on it.'

**571.** My husband has solutions to every problem. For example, he says the easiest way to remove red wine stains from a white silk dress is with a pair of scissors.

**572.** My neighbour is lucky. Her husband uses paint that doesn't drip to decorate the house, whereas I'm married to a drip who doesn't paint.

**573.** What can a wife say to her husband just after they've made love?

Anything she likes as he's fast asleep.

**574.** When I'm in bed with my husband I find that one good turn can get all the blankets.

**575.** Last night my husband saw a horror film that scared him half to death. He's now worried in case he sees another one.

**576.** Whenever my husband has to fill in a form giving details of 'person to notify in case of accident', he always writes: 'The nearest doctor.'

**577.** When Helga paid an unexpected visit on her friend, Martha, she found Martha in a rather flustered state. 'I've just buried my husband,' explained Martha.

'Oh dear,' said Helga. 'But what happened to your clothes – they're all torn. And your hands and face are badly scratched.'

'I know,' replied Martha. 'It wasn't easy to bury him. Even after I hit him on the head with a spade he fought like mad.'

**578.** My husband thinks that an IQ test is a lot of people being asked difficult questions while they stand in line outside an optician's.

**579.** My husband is a light eater – as soon as it's light he starts eating.

**580.** In a fight, some people use their fists. My husband uses his feet – he runs away as fast as possible.

**581.** She came home from work to find her rather naïve husband wearing her raincoat underneath his overcoat – and he was painting the lounge.

'Why are you dressed like that to do some decorating?' she asked.

'I'm just following the direction on the paint tin,' he replied. 'For best results, put on two coats.'

**582.** James went to a counsellor and said, 'I hope you can help me. My wife is very unfaithful. Every evening she goes out to the same bar and picks up men. She'll have sex with anyone who asks her – no matter what they look like. What can I do?'

The counsellor looked at James and said, 'Don't worry. Now, what was the name of that bar?'

**583.** The greatest cause of divorce is marriage.

**584.** His mistress has the same first name as his wife. This was a deliberate safety measure on his part – in case he talks in his sleep.

**585.** When his wife asked him why he kept coming home half drunk he replied that he never had enough money to get completely drunk.

**586.** When Mavis was warned by her doctor not to touch anything alcoholic she told her husband not to go anywhere near her.

**587.** I wouldn't say he's hen-pecked – just spouse-broken.

**588.** Wendy was sobbing as she phoned her best friend, Louise. 'It's my husband,' cried Wendy. 'He's just died.'

'Oh, I'm terribly sorry,' said Louise. 'Were you with him when he died?'

'Yes,' sobbed Wendy. 'I don't know what to do.'

'It must be terrible for you,' said Louise. 'Did he have any last requests?'

'Yes,' sobbed Wendy. 'He looked at me and asked: 'Please put down that gun. Please don't shoot me ...'

**589.** He's so stupid that whenever he paints the house his wife has to take precautions to stop him from hurting himself. She puts a 'Stop' sign on the top rung of his ladder.

**590.** He likes to help his wife with the housework – he lifts his legs up on to the sofa when she wants to vacuum the carpet.

**591.** Her husband is a transvestite. He likes to eat, drink and be Mary.

**592.** My husband keeps saying he's suffering from hallucinations – but I'm sure he's just imagining it.

**593.** My husband used to run a flea circus. He started it from scratch.

**594.** My friend Elaine told me at lunch that she had to be especially careful not to get pregnant. I was surprised.

'Hasn't your husband just had a vasectomy?' I asked.

'Yes,' replied Elaine, eyeing an attractive waiter. 'That's why I've got to be careful.'

**595.** Last night he rushed home and told his wife, 'I've just found a fantastic job. Excellent pay, good holidays and excellent prospects. But hard work is expected.'

'Wonderful,' said his wife.

'Yes,' said the man. 'You start next week.'


**596.** When I asked him how he had got a large bruise on his cheek, he told me it was caused by a glancing blow. He had been out shopping with his wife when he had glanced at a beautiful woman. His wife hit him.


**597.** We've been married ten years and never a cross word – my wife cuts them out of the newspaper so I can never do them.


**598.** Nigel was distraught. He had received an anonymous phone call at his office, telling him that his wife was having an affair with a man who worked for a pest control company.

Nigel rushed home to discover a pest control van in his driveway. He let himself into the house. There was no sign of his wife. Then he walked up the stairs and heard sounds of feverish activity.

Flinging open the bedroom door he saw his wife zipping up her dress.

'You're home early, dear,' said his wife. 'I was just putting on some clean clothes. The others got messed up when I was showing the pest control man the attic.'

'Where is he now?' asked Nigel.

'I'm not too sure,' replied the wife.

Nigel looked around the bedroom and opened a cupboard. Standing inside was a naked man.

'What is the meaning of this?' demanded Nigel.

'Well,' replied the naked man. 'After looking for woodworm in the loft I thought there might be an infestation of moths in the bedroom.'

'Where are your clothes?' asked Nigel.

The naked man looked down at himself, appeared to be astonished, and exclaimed: 'Those blasted moths must have eaten them!'

**599.** The hen-pecked husband could stand it no more.

'I'm off to join the Foreign Legion,' he said to his wife as he packed a suitcase.

His wife looked at him with a sneer and said: 'Well, when you get back make sure you take off your shoes before coming into the house. I don't want sandy footprints all over the carpet!'

**600.** When Robert came home unexpectedly early from work one day he found his wife in bed with another man. 'How dare you!' shouted Robert at his wife. 'Who *is* this man?'

Robert's wife replied. 'We only met at lunchtime. I forgot to ask his name.'

**601.** They have been married for twenty-five years – and they are still in love: he with his secretary, and she with the gardener.

**602.** My wife lets me run things around the house – the washing machine, vacuum cleaner and dishwasher.

**603.** His marriage is based on trust and understanding. She doesn't trust him – and he can't understand her.

**604.** When Sally came home from work her husband said, 'Let's go out and have some fun tonight.'

'Good idea,' replied Sally. 'But if you get home before I do, remember not to put the chain on the front door.'


**605.** If it is true that love is blind – then marriage is certainly an eye-opener.


**606.** My wife believes in an open marriage – she opens my mail, and my wallet.


**607.** His son asked him, 'How much does it cost to get married?' He replied, 'I don't really know – I'm still paying for it.'


**608.** There are only two times in a man's life when he won't be able to understand women – the time when he's single and the time when he's married.


**609.** There are a lot of pathetic jokes in the world. I should know – I married one of them.


**610.** When John made his girlfriend pregnant, her father sent two large, powerful men to his office to discuss John's marriage – it was a wife or death situation.

**611.** My brother-in-law broke up my marriage – my husband came home early one day and found me in bed with him.


**612.** David's wife was in tears. 'What's wrong?' he asked. 'It's our daughter Fiona,' sobbed the wife. 'I know she's in love with Mike and they'll make a lovely couple. But she's only 20 and when she marries she'll leave home and …'

'There, there,' soothed David. 'I know we'll be losing a daughter but we'll be gaining a bathroom and a telephone.'


**613.** She got all excited about nothing – and then married him.


**614.** Before they married, he told his wife-to-be that he would climb the highest mountain, swim the largest ocean and trek across the North Pole for her. After two years of marriage she divorced him because he was always away from home.


**615.** The secret of their long and happy marriage is that three times a week they go out for a romantic meal – he with his mistress, and she with her lover.


**616.** Claude and his wife were having an argument over the solution to a crossword clue.

'I *know* my answer is right,' said Claude. 'I'm not a *complete* idiot!'

'Really?' sneered his wife. 'Which part of you is missing?'

**617.** Uncle Clive is my *dearest* relative. He's been married eight times – and each time I've had to buy him a wedding present.

**618.** Last night she had a man in her bed gasping for breath and calling her name. She was trying to smother her husband with a pillow.

**619.** My husband is an incredible man. He doesn't know the meaning of fear, defeat or surrender – so I've bought him a dictionary.

**620.** My husband's in the army. He keeps being posted abroad and I hardly ever see him. In fact, I'm worried I won't recognise him when he turns up on the doorstep expecting a romantic welcome. That's why I have to kiss passionately every man who comes to the door.

**621.** One of the disadvantages of polygamy is the hours a husband must wait trying to get into the bathroom.

**622.** 'Darling', he said to his wife. 'What would you like for your birthday? A new car? A round-the-world holiday?'

'None of those things,' replied his wife. 'I want a divorce.'

'Oh!' he replied. 'I wasn't intending to spend that much.'

**623.** Last night in a bar I overheard a man talking to a young woman. He said, 'Having sex with my wife is like Valentine's Day.'

The woman said, 'That sounds as if it's wonderfully romantic.'

'No,' replied the man, 'It only happens once a year.'

**624.** Jeremy and his wife are sexually compatible – every night they both have headaches.

**625.** His wife told him he should be much more loving – so he went and got two mistresses.

**626.** I'd like to thank my Uncle Paul for the wonderful wedding present of a 50-piece dinner set. The box of wooden toothpicks will be really useful.

**627.** This is a very emotional wedding – even the cake is in tiers.

**628.** His wife has still got her wedding outfit – the beautiful white dress, the veil – and the shotgun.

**629.** I would like to thank my mother-in-law for the wonderful present – a set of towels marked 'Hers' and 'Thing'.

**630.** The couple had just celebrated their fiftieth wedding anniversary. Just as they were about to go to bed, a fairy suddenly appeared and said, 'I am a good fairy. You have both been such a good couple for so many years that I can grant you one wish each.'

The fairy turned to the wife and asked, 'What would you like?'

'A sack full of money,' said the woman. There was a puff of smoke and the sack of money appeared. The woman was delighted and started to count the money.

Her husband approached the fairy and whispered, 'For my wish, I would like to have a woman much younger than me.'

There was a puff of smoke, and the man found himself lying on the floor. He was twenty years older.

**631.** His wife has an even temper – she's always angry.

**632.** My wife is like a wild animal in bed – she snores like a hippo.

**633.** His wife would look good in something long and flowing – like the Nile or the Amazon.

**634.** He's a very happy man with a wife who is fantastic in bed and a wife who cooks superb meals and does his laundry. He just hopes the two women never meet.

**635.** He said he realised how much his wife loved him when he unexpectedly fell ill and could not go to work for three days. His wife was so pleased to have him at home that she told everyone about it. Every time the phone rang she started off by saying, 'My husband's at home.' Whenever anyone started walking up the path to his front door – such as the newspaper deliverer, milkman, postman and gardener – she rushed out saying, 'My husband's at home!'

**636.** When I told my wife I'd met a man who rowed across the Atlantic single-handed, she asked: 'Why didn't he use both hands?'

**637.** My wife likes to pick up a good book and not put it down until she's finished. Unfortunately, it's my cheque book.

**638.** The only time my wife pays any attention to what I am saying is when I talk in my sleep.

**639.** He can talk to his wife about anything – politics, philosophy, music, sport, religion, books, art – absolutely anything. She won't understand it – but he can talk to her about it.

**640.** My wife is very dear to me – with all the stuff she buys she costs me a fortune.

**641.** My wife is so silly. She thinks a lump sum investment policy only pays out if she gets lumps.

**642.** Lots of women say they want a man's salary. My wife already gets one – she takes all of mine.

**643.** A friend of mine has just spent £10,000 on a little peace and quiet. His little piece wanted the £10,000 to keep it quiet from his wife.

**644.** The husband was furious. 'Is it true you've been having an affair with John?' he angrily asked his wife.

'Yes,' replied the wife.

'Then,' said the husband, 'I'm going round to his house and I'll teach him a lesson . . .'

'But darling,' said the wife, 'couldn't you take a few lessons from him instead and then I wouldn't need to have an affair?'

**645.** When my husband was born, it wasn't a stork that delivered him – it was a vulture.

**646.** My wife refuses to use Inter Flora for people's birthdays. She says she doesn't think people would like margarine as a present.

**647.** It's my wife's birthday tomorrow. Last week I asked her what she wanted as a present.

'Oh, I don't know,' she said. 'Just give me something with diamonds.'

That's why I'm giving her a pack of playing cards.

**648.** My wife is the only person I know who can ruin cornflakes – she boils them in the packet.

**649.** 'Darling,' called the young bride from the kitchen. 'I'm afraid I've spoilt your breakfast. The eggs were frying nicely when all of a sudden the shells broke and it all became very messy.'

**650.** My husband's cooking is so bad he's even managed to give the dustbin food poisoning.

**651.** There's only two things wrong with my husband's dancing – his left foot and his right foot.

**652.** A friend of mine has just got divorced due to incompatibility. He had no income and his wife had no pat-ability.

**653.** In olden days England, the unfaithful princess was divorced because she had lots of sleepless knights.

**654.** A couple I used to know recently got divorced and they fought over the custody of their teenage children – neither of them wanted custody.

**655.** Their marriage broke up because he was always leaving the house after shouting a four-letter word at his wife: 'Golf' or 'Work'.

**656.** My husband wanted his fortune told, but didn't know whether to go to a mindreader or a palmist. I told him to go to a palmist – at least we know he's got a palm.

**657.** 'Darling, just imagine – we've now been married for twenty-four hours.'

'Yes, dear, it's incredible. And it seems only as if it was yesterday.'

**658.** As they lay in bed on the first day of their honeymoon, John turned to his wife and sighed, 'Darling, I hope you can put up with my ugly face for the rest of your life.'

'That's all right, dear,' she replied. 'You'll be out at work all day.'

**659.** Mabel is the best housekeeper in the world. She's been divorced fifteen times – and each time she's kept the house.

**660.** For twenty-two years my husband and I were happy – then we met and got married.

**661.** My husband used to be a professional violinist, but he had to give it up because it gave him a bad back. It was all the bending down to pick up the coins in the hat that did it ...

**662.** The other day I saw my husband facing a mirror with his eyes closed. I asked him what he was doing and he said he was trying to see what he looked like when he was asleep.

**663.** My husband is a very noisy eater. Last night we went to an exclusive, cosy little nightclub and when he drank his soup five couples got up to dance the cha-cha.

**664.** When I asked my husband why he parted his hair in the middle, he replied, 'It's so my head will be evenly balanced.'

**665.** Someone once asked me if I believed in clubs for promiscuous husbands. I said that poison was safer than using a club.

**666.** My husband is so pedantic. If you say to him, 'How do you do?', he'll reply, 'Do what?'

**667.** My husband is so thin and has such a gigantic nose and enormous ears that whenever he stands up in a restaurant people hang their coats and hats on him.

**668.** My husband is so stupid that when I gave birth to triplets, he wanted to know who the other two fathers were.

**669.** Last year the children and I had a lot of fun on holiday burying my husband in the sand on the beach. Next year we might go back and dig him up.

**670.** I know my husband's hair is all his own – I went with him when he made the final payment on his wig.

**671.** I have a special soft spot for my husband – a large swamp in Africa.

**672.** I don't know what to make of my husband. I suppose if I was a cannibal I could make him into a casserole.

**673.** My sister has had five husbands – two of her own, and three married to friends.

**674.** I like to make my husband laugh on New Year's Day so I tell him jokes on Boxing Day.

**675.** My husband is a regular churchgoer – he never misses the Christmas Eve service.

**676.** My husband wanted to be a tree surgeon when he was young – but he couldn't stand the sight of sap.

**677.** My husband has finally given up eating Smarties. He said it took too long to peel off the shells to get to the chocolate.

**678.** My husband has got such a long face that his barber charges him double for shaving it.

**679.** My husband keeps pining for his lost youth – he lost her to another boy at school.

**680.** My husband is so stupid. When I told him the car battery was dead, he took it out and buried it.

**681.** When my husband told me that his pot belly had got a lot smaller, I told him it was only wishful shrinking.

**682.** My sister has just lost two hundred pounds of ugly fat – her husband left her.

**683.** Last year when I was on holiday in the USA I bought a lovely chair for my husband. Now all I've got to do is plug it in.

**684.** My husband isn't a hard drinker – he finds it very easy.

**685.** My husband has more chins than a Chinese telephone book.

**686.** People keep asking me if I mind that my husband chases after pretty young women. I tell them that it's a bit like dogs chasing after cars – they wouldn't know what to do if they caught one.

**687.** You can always tell when my husband has just told a joke at a party – the whole room goes deathly quiet.

**688.** My husband was such an ugly baby that his mother refused to push him in his pram – she pulled it.

**689.** I think I have the perfect husband. Pity I'm not married to him.

**690.** My husband can charm the birds out of the trees – vultures, crows, buzzards ...

**691.** My husband says he is a man with many hidden talents. I suppose one day he might find one of them.

**692.** Fred came home early from work one day and found his wife in bed with the postman.
    'What on earth do you think you're doing?' demanded Fred.

'I see what you mean,' said the postman to Fred's wife, continuing his exertions. 'He really is as stupid as you said he is, if he has to ask a question like that!'

**693.** My wife was knitting the most peculiar garment last week. It had lots of strings at the top and a huge canopy. She said it was a parachute jumper.

**694.** The Browns were a wealthy middle-aged couple who lived in a large house in the country. All went well for many years until a new maid arrived. She was extremely attractive. Within six months of her arrival, Mr Brown was starting to wake up every morning at 5 am instead of his usual 7.30 am.

'Where are you going?' Mrs Brown would ask, as her husband got out of bed and slipped on his dressing gown.

'Once awake, I can't get back to sleep,' Mr Brown replied, 'so I think I'll do some work in my study or walk around the garden. You don't need to get up – just go back to sleep. You know how deep sleep keeps you beautiful.'

Mrs Brown began to suspect that her husband was sneaking into the maid's room. What should she do?

It was soon to be the maid's parents' wedding anniversary, so one Thursday afternoon when Mr Brown was on a business trip to London, Mrs Brown suggested that the maid might like to pay a surprise visit to her parents.

'You can go now, if you like,' suggested Mrs Brown, 'and come back on Monday.'

'Thanks very much,' said the maid, 'it's most kind of you.' And she went off to pack for her trip.

Soon the maid had left the house. Mr Brown returned around 9 pm and, after watching TV for a bit, went to bed.

Promptly at 5 am, Mr Brown woke up and said he couldn't sleep any more and was going for a stroll around the garden.

As soon as her husband left the room, and she could hear him cleaning his teeth in the bathroom, Mrs Brown rushed to the maid's room and got into the maid's bed.

Mrs Brown had been lying in the dark for about five minutes when she heard the sash window of the room being slowly lifted and a man climbed in through the window.

Mrs Brown tensed herself in the darkness, but relaxed as the man made tender, passionate love to her. She was ecstatic. Why could her husband make such wonderful love to the maid and be so boring in bed with her?

'Darling,' whispered Mrs Brown, snuggling up to the man in bed, 'let's do it again.'

'Sorry, luv,' replied the man. Mrs Brown was aghast. It was not her husband's voice. 'No time for more now,' continued the man, 'but I can come back when I've finished the milk round.'

**695.** After we got married, I no longer had buttons missing from my shirts, and my clothes were no longer creased – my wife taught me how to sew and iron!

**696.** They were a well-matched couple as both of them were madly in love – she with herself, and he with himself.

**697.** My sister has just married for the fourth time. Her first husband was very wealthy. Her second husband was a theatrical producer and she wanted to be in one of his musicals. Her third husband liked donkeys – and she'd always wanted a donkey. And her current husband is Japanese and likes playing a game for two.

In fact, as far as husbands go, she's had one for the money, two for the show, three to get neddy, and four to play Go!

**698.** People keep saying that two can live as cheaply as one – but they never seem to finish the sentence: one *what*?

**699.** I married my husband because I thought he was rich. He said he owned a chain of newspapers.

The day after we married, he took me up to the attic of his mother's house and showed me what he did when he was a small boy at school – made a chain out of old newspapers.

**700.** The only reason Henrietta married Archibald was because he gave her an engagement ring, and she grew too fat to be able to get it off her finger and give it back to him.

**701.** I once knew a man who was so mean he spent years and years before he found his ideal wife – a woman born on the 29th February so he would only have to buy her a birthday card every four years.

**702.** I can marry anyone I please. Trouble is, I haven't pleased anyone yet.

**703.** In many marriages, there have been three rings: an engagement ring, a wedding ring – and suffering.

**704.** I was sitting on a train to London the other day when I overhead two young girls talking.

One girl said, 'Last night, Julian told me that he wanted to marry the cleverest, most beautiful girl in the world.'

'Oh,' replied the other girl, 'that's pity. He's been your boyfriend for at least two years and now he says he's going to marry someone else.'

**705.** I married my wealthy husband because he said if I did he would be humbly grateful. Instead, he's been grumbly hateful.

**706.** For the whole of the first week of our marriage, my wife went to bed every night wearing a white glove on her left hand, and a small white sock on her left foot. I thought this was rather odd, but didn't like to ask her about it until the second week when I eventually plucked up courage.

'Darling,' said my demure bride, 'my mother said that if I wanted a long and happy marriage, I should keep an air of mystery and never let you see me completely naked!'

**707.** 'My mother-in-law has gone to the West Indies.'

'Jamaica?'

'No – she decided to go by herself.'

**708.** My mother-in-law is very spiteful. When she caught rabies, she wrote down a list of people she wanted to bite.

**709.** They did things differently when my mother-in-law was a girl – otherwise they'd never have classified her as a girl.

**710.** 'My mother-in-law has gone to Indonesia.'
'Jakarta?'
'No – she went by plane.'

**711.** Fred: My mother-in-law arrived unexpectedly last night and since we were short of beds she had to sleep in the bath. But the stupid woman fell asleep and left the water running.

Tom: Did the bath overflow?

Fred: No. My mother-in-law always sleeps with her mouth open.

**712.** You can tell when his wife is starting to get tired – she can hardly keep her mouth open.

**713.** 'I say, old man,' said Alan to the host of the party, 'there's this rather delectable young chick whom I'm getting along really well with, if you know what I mean.' He winked, and continued, 'And I wondered if I might use your spare bedroom for a short while.'

'No, I don't mind,' replied the host, 'but what about your wife?'

'Oh, don't bother about her,' said Alan. 'I'll only be gone a short time and I'm sure she won't miss me.'

'I *know* she won't miss you,' stated the host, 'it's only five minutes ago that *she* borrowed the spare bedroom!'

**714.** When my husband complained that his new passport photo didn't do him justice, I told him that he didn't really want justice – he needed mercy.

**715.** Albert was disappointed with his wife. Almost every night she had a headache, or was too tired, or made some other excuse not to make love.

In desperation, knowing how much his wife loved money, he told her, 'I'll put a £10 note in the top drawer of your dressing table every time we make love.'

Soon, Albert was happy and his wife delighted in taking the £10 notes from him for her passionate work.

Then one day Albert happened to open the top drawer of the dressing table and saw a bundle of £10 notes and another bundle of £20 notes – plus a number of £50 notes.

'Where did all this money come from?' asked Albert. 'I only give you £10 notes.'

'Well, dear,' said his wife, 'not everyone is as mean as you.'

**716.** When Sally came home from the office unexpectedly early one day she found her handsome young husband in bed with a 65-year-old woman. Sally was horrified.

Sally's husband looked up at her and said, 'Darling, this is the lady who provided your Porsche, and that nice diamond ring I gave you last week, and …'

'Oh,' said Sally. 'Sorry I interrupted. And can I have a necklace to match my ring?'


**717.** Mrs Green was outraged. She had caught the nubile young cook kissing and cuddling in the kitchen with Mr Green.

'If it happens again,' said Mrs Green, 'I'll have to get another cook.'

'Oh,' replied the cook, 'I wish you would. Your husband's always said he fancied it with two of us.'


**718.** My marriage to Charles was a mistake. When he was just a boyfriend, I thought he said he was over-sexed. Now I'm married to him, I realise I must have misheard him say he was over sex.


**719.** When I asked a friend of mine if he ever woke up grumpy in the morning, he said that he didn't have to – his wife had her own alarm clock.


**720.** Mr Smith was fed up with his wife's insistence on absolute tidiness. He was not allowed to smoke cigarettes or cigars or a pipe at home. He had to take off his shoes before he entered the house.

His wife even made him comb his hair in the garden in case a spot of dandruff fell on the floor.

When he died, Mr Smith managed to get some revenge. His will stipulated that his ashes were to be scattered on the lounge carpet.

**721.** The hard-pressed managing director had just returned from a gruelling overseas trip and was relaxing at home when the telephone rang. When he hung up almost at once, his wife enquired who it was.

'Someone with the wrong number, my love,' he said. 'He wanted to know if the coast was clear. So I suggested he telephone the Met Office!'

**722.** I was a bit concerned on our wedding day when my husband stumbled over the words of his wedding vows, dropped the ring, and then whispered to the best man, 'Sorry! I'll do better next time.'

**723.** What is the point of being best man if you never get a chance to prove it?

**724.** It was the woman's second marriage, and her first husband was kind enough to send the happy couple a wedding gift of a carving set – two chisels and a hammer.

**725.** I used to miss my wife every time she went away for a week to visit her mother. But now I just get a neighbour to nag me instead.

**726.** My wife isn't exactly fat and ugly, but whenever she goes to the doctor he tells her to open her mouth and say 'Moo!'

**727.** I call my wife a wonder woman – I sometimes wonder if she's a woman.

**728.** If my wife has nothing to wear, why does she need three giant wardrobes to keep it in?

**729.** My wife makes a good living curing people. She's so ugly she hires herself out to frighten people and cure them of hiccups.

**730.** Claude's wife is like the Mona Lisa – she's as flat as a canvas and should be in a museum.

**731.** My husband says he's going to dance on my grave when I die – so today I made a new will leaving instructions that I'm to be buried at sea.

**732.** My wife is a wonderful magician – she can turn anything into an argument.

**733.** My wife is so jealous that when she couldn't find any female hairs on my coat, she accused me of going out with bald-headed women.

**734.** I wouldn't say my wife has a big mouth, but she called me from London yesterday. I was in Southampton at the time and we don't *have* a telephone!

**735.** It's not that my wife was fat when I married her – it's just that when I carried her over the threshold, I had to make two trips.

**736.** My wife has a stomach problem – she's grown so fat she can't fasten her blouse over her stomach.

**737.** Last night at the dinner party my wife gave me a terrible kick that has left a nasty bruise. All I did was whisper to her that I thought her white tights looked a bit wrinkled. Unfortunately, she wasn't wearing any tights.

**738.** The easiest way to stop a runaway horse is to get my wife to place a bet on it.

**739.** The much-married actor told his new girlfriend that she shouldn't believe all the tales about his bad habits – they were just old wives' tales.

**740.** I've had to wear pink frilly knickers ever since my wife discovered a pair in my raincoat pocket.

**741.** I think I've rather dropped myself in it. Early this morning, when I was not properly awake, my wife said, 'Darling, what would you do if I died?'

I stretched, yawned and said, 'I don't know, dear. I love you too much to want to think about awful things like that – especially so early in the morning.'

'But what would you do? Would you remarry?' asked my wife.

'I don't think so, dear,' I replied. 'You know I only have eyes for you. Who could possibly be as wonderful as you?'

I yawned again and then tried to go back to sleep for another few minutes, but my wife continued her questions. 'If you did remarry,' she said, 'would your new wife wear my rings and necklaces?'

'I don't think so,' I said, without thinking. 'Aurelia's got smaller fingers and a more delicate neck than you, dear.'

**742.** My wife has a better sense of judgment than I have – she chose me as her husband.

**743.** My wife is so ugly. When we went on holiday to Africa even the mosquitoes wouldn't bite her.

**744.** My wife is thinking about going back to university. She's just heard that they've got a new course which she thinks is all about shopping – it's called buy-ology.

**745.** My wife is so ugly that last night I got a phone call from a Peeping Tom pleading with me to get her to close the curtains before she undresses for bed.

**746.** My wife is so stupid she once took a tape measure to bed with her to try and discover how long she slept.

**747.** I wouldn't say my wife is a gossip – she just has a good sense of rumour.

**748.** My wife has a very clean mind – probably because she changes it every few minutes.

**749.** My wife has a photographic mind – but it's a great pity it never developed.

**750.** My wife is so conceited she only looks at me because she can see her own reflection in my spectacles.

**751.** My wife is so ugly whenever she goes to the zoo, she has to buy two tickets – one to get in, and one to get out.

**752.** My wife has a memory like an elephant – and a face to match.

**753.** My wife was so bad when she was a small girl that her parents ran away from home.

**754.** My wife is in the mining business – she's always saying, 'That's mine! That's mine! And that's mine!'

**755.** My wife doesn't really have a big mouth – but she once gave the kiss of life to a whale.

**756.** It was breakfast one month after their marriage.

'Darling,' said the wife. 'Will you love me when I'm old and wrinkled.'

The husband lowered his morning newspaper and said, 'Of course, I do.'


**757.** When Fred's wife was born, they fired 21 guns. Unfortunately, they all missed.


**758.** He hasn't spoken to his wife for the past six months – she hates to be interrupted.


**759.** He knew he was addicted to the internet, when he banged on the bathroom door and told his wife he urgently needed the toilet as he wanted to download.

# MONEY

**760.** It is better to borrow money from pessimists rather than optimists. Pessimists are less likely to expect repayment.

**761.** He's tried hard to budget – but at the end of the money he always has some month left.

**762.** Every time I think I can make ends meet they move the ends.

**763.** The difference between creditors and debtors is that debtors *know* they owe money, whereas most creditors *think* they are going to get the money they are owed.

**764.** A lot of young women treat him as a father figure – they ask him for money.

**765.** If money talks, then why does so much of it seem to say 'goodbye'?

**766.** Money can't buy love. But it *can* hire a good imitation.

**767.** The greatest difference between death and taxes is that death doesn't get worse every time the Government presents its Budget.

**768.** The problem with income tax forms is that it takes more time and effort to fill in the forms than it does to earn the income.

**769.** 'Why,' asked Mr White, 'are you still overdrawn at the bank?'

'I don't know,' replied his wife. 'They sent me a bank statement last month and a letter saying I was £500 overdrawn. Then they sent me another letter insisting I pay the £500 within seven days. So I paid it promptly. I immediately sent them a cheque for the money.'

**770.** Insurance agent: Now, madam, this policy is a particularly good buy. Under it, we pay up to £5,000 for broken arms or legs.

Woman: But what do you do with them all?

**771.** Are stockbrokers so called because they sell you stock that makes you broke?

**772.** With so much uncertainty in the Stock Market, many investors are no longer bulls or bears – they're chickens or lemmings.

**773.** A friend once asked me for some investment advice. I asked him if he had any liquid assets. He said he did – three bottles of Scotch and a can of fizzy orange.

**774.** I once knew a Japanese gentleman who was so wealthy that he was considering buying himself what he called 'a place down South'. It was Australia.

**775.** An elderly miser was passing an undertaker's when he noticed that they were having a 'cut price funeral offer' – so he went in and ordered one, then went home and committed suicide.

**776.** The rich, miserly lady discovered that her husband had died during the night. She wondered for a moment how to break the news to the servants. Then she rang her bell for the maid.

'Josephine,' said the thrifty lady, 'you need only boil *one* egg for breakfast.'

**777.** I once knew a man who was so miserly that he said he wouldn't want to buy a nuclear fall-out shelter now because it was cheaper to wait and get one second-hand.

**778.** The miser was so mean he even re-used the toilet paper.

**779.** The mean, wealthy lady was walking along a fashionable street in London when an unemployed young man begged her for money.

'I'm homeless, jobless and I'm starving,' said the man. 'Please give me a few pounds for some soup.'

'You can get soup for less than that!' snapped the lady.

'I know,' said the young man, 'but I have to give the waiter a good tip.'

**780.** Years ago, Mr Smith gave his wife a large strong box and encouraged her to put something away for a rainy day. When she died, Mr Smith opened the box – and found seven umbrellas, six pairs of Wellington boots and fourteen raincoats.

# PEOPLE

**781.** Cameron was walking home after working late at the office when a beggar made an impassioned plea to him that he felt unable to refuse.

'Please sir,' said the beggar. 'Please help me with some money. I have a wife and family and a pet dog to support and all I have are these ragged old clothes – and this loaded gun in my pocket.'

**782.** I was walking along the beach this morning when I saw a man standing on top of the cliff. He put a small bird on each shoulder, and then jumped over the edge. As I raced towards his crumpled body, he moaned, 'My friend said that budgie jumping was safe!'

**783.** He boasted that no matter what happened to him, he always managed to keep his head above water. For him it was quite easy – wood floats.

**784.** The man in the bar was boasting, 'The woman who marries my son will get a great prize.'

Hearing this, a young woman asked, 'What prize exactly would you give me if I married him?'

**785.** Every time he reminisces about his past achievements I am constantly amazed. It seems the older he gets, the better he used to be.

**786.** George was delighted the day he got his first set of false teeth. Even his young children said the teeth made him look years younger.

That evening George had a lot of work to do in his study, so by the time he went to bed he was feeling very tired. As he bent towards the bedside table to set his alarm clock, George realised he was still wearing his false teeth. He felt too weary to get out of bed and go to the bathroom to put the teeth in a glass of water, so he just removed the teeth and put them on the bedside table.

The following morning the teeth had disappeared. George looked behind the bedside table, under the bed, queried the children as to the whereabouts of his missing teeth – but the teeth could not be found.

Later that day he was making his bed and, lifting up the pillow, saw a pile of coins resting on the sheet. The tooth fairy had taken his false teeth by mistake.

**787.** He was just about to be shot by a firing squad when the rebel leader asked him, 'Do you have any last requests?'

'Yes,' replied the captive. 'Can I sing a song?'

The rebel leader thought for a few seconds, then said, 'OK. Start singing.'

The captive started: 'There were ten million green bottles standing on a wall ...'

**788.** Bernard was standing with his back to a wall. Facing him was a firing squad.

'Would you like a cigarette?' asked the leader of the firing squad.

'No thanks,' replied Bernard. 'I'm giving them up for health reasons.'

**789.** Two men were captured by rebels and were to be killed by firing squad. The rebel leader kicked one of the captured men and said, 'You are first to be shot. Do you have any last requests?'

'Yes, said the man. 'I love rap music. Can you play one of the rap CDs you took from my bag over your loudspeaker system?'

The rebel leader replied, 'We can do that. In fact, I quite like rap music myself. Maybe we can play two or three tracks.'

The second captured man then said, 'Please! If you are going to do that, then my last request is to be shot first.'


**790.** Last week I was walking along the beach when I saw an old bottle sticking out of the sand. Fearing it might cause someone to trip, I pulled it from the sand and as I did so the top came off the bottle and an elderly genie popped out.

'How can I help you?' asked the genie. 'I have been stuck in this bottle for many, many years as the waves carried me many miles.'

'Do I get three wishes?' I asked.

'Sorry,' replied the genie. 'I am so old most of my powers have gone. I no longer have the power to give you eternal life or a fortune in gold. But I could probably manage a more modest request.'

'How about a date with an attractive film star?' I asked.

'Certainly!' replied the genie. 'It is done' – and he vanished in a puff of smoke.

Two days later a large limousine drew up outside my house, a uniformed chauffeur got out and said he was taking me to town for a surprise meeting with a film star. I was really excited throughout the journey. On arrival at an expensive hotel I was escorted to a suite where, lying on a sofa, was my date – Lassie.

**791.** James and Keith went on a hunting holiday. On their second day they were walking in the woods when they suddenly realised they were lost. They sat and thought about their predicament.

Keith said, 'I remember from my granddad that the best way to get someone to come and rescue you is to fire three times in the air.'

'Good idea,' said James, and fired three times.

Thirty minutes later, there were no sounds of any rescuers so James fired again. Still no sounds of rescue.

After a further thirty minutes they fired three more times and Keith said, 'I hope a guide or some rescuers come soon – we've only got three more arrows left.'

**792.** Nowadays, it's not people who send poison pen letters that you have to worry about – but those obnoxious people who make disgusting comments via the internet. Indeed, the e-mail of the species is deadlier than the mail.

**793.** Old mailmen never die – they just get another posting.

**794.** I'm not very good in the morning until after I've had breakfast. For example, when I got up this morning I staggered to the bathroom, stared in the mirror and wondered where I'd seen that face before.

**795.** What do you give a man who has all the latest high-tech gadgets?

The services of a six-year-old boy to show him how to work them all.

**796.** When he told me he was a self-made man I said it was very honest of him to take all the blame.

**797.** He was a self-made man. Unfortunately, he quit before he'd finished.

**798.** One of the great mysteries of life is why is it that when you share a bedroom, the person who goes to sleep first is always the one who snores?

**799.** One applicant for a media studies course was asked by a university tutor, 'If you could interview anyone, living or dead, who would you interview?'
The applicant replied, 'The living one.'

**800.** He recently painted the sundial in his garden. He used luminous paint because he said he wanted to be able to tell the time at night.

**801.** A bore is someone who opens his mouth and puts his own feats in it.

**802.** Bores are people who don't know that the best speeches are like a well-kept lawn: short and neat.

**803.** There is an ancient Chinese ceremony in which the parents of a child choose the baby's name.

As soon as the baby is born, all the cutlery in the house of its parents is thrown in the air. The parents then listen to the falling knives, forks and spoons and choose a name: ping, chang, fan, fung, cheung ...

**804.** When I told the trainee decorator that I wanted a matt finish on the walls, he nailed the carpets to them.

**805.** Man on phone: Help! Come quickly! My house is on fire!

Fire brigade officer: How do we get to your house?

Man on phone: What? Don't you still have those big red trucks?

**806.** The hereditary peer was boasting of his ancestors and generally acting in an arrogant and disdainful manner towards one of his fellow club members who was a self-made man.

Eventually, the man could stand the peer's attitude no longer and said, in a loud voice, 'From what you have been saying, it would appear that the nobility of my family begins with me, whereas that of yours ended with your father.'

**807.** It was an international television conference in the USA and the delegates were eating the farewell dinner of the conference.

A Japanese gentleman was sitting next to a delegate from Portland, Oregon. After the Japanese had finished his soup, the American asked him, 'Likee soupee?' The Japanese gentleman nodded.

Throughout the meal, the American asked such questions as, 'Likee fishee?' and 'Likee drinkee?'

When the meal was finished, the chairman of the conference rose to his feet and introduced the Japanese gentleman as the guest speaker of the meeting.

The Oriental gentleman gave a witty, excellent speech on the future of broadcasting – speaking in English much better than anything the man from Oregon could manage.

After his speech, the Japanese gentleman returned to his seat and asked his American table companion, 'Likee speechee?'


**808.** I once knew a man who was sold a plot of land at the North Pole. He thought it was the ideal place to grow frozen peas.


**809.** The gorgeous new maid had once been a gymnast in Romania. She was now trying to improve her English by working for Lord and Lady Spiffleburgson at their mansion in Dorset.

The maid had been with the Spiffleburgsons for only nine days and found many English habits rather strange. But she was determined to succeed as she desperately needed her salary to help support her family in Romania.

Thus it was that at a luncheon party at the mansion she walked in, carefully carrying a large bowl of salad – but the guests were rather astonished that she was completely naked.

The gentlemen at the luncheon raised their eyebrows while secretly admiring her trim, lithe young body, while the ladies demurely tried to look away.

After the maid had placed the bowl of salad on the table and was leaving the room, Lady Spiffleburgson rose from her chair and accompanied the maid to the kitchen.

'My dear,' said her ladyship, 'why are you walking about naked?'

'I only obey your orders,' said the maid. 'I hear you say – you say several times – and you say it important for me to remember – I must serve salad without dressing.'

**810.** You've only got to look at popular sayings to know that it's true that women are more intelligent than men. For example, 'Diamonds are a girl's best friend' but 'A man's best friend is his dog.'

**811.** The poet had been boring everyone at the party by droning on and on about his various sources of inspiration and how he was trying to write a poem composed of distichs in elegiac form.

Towards the end of the party, he approached a sweet young girl and said, 'You know, I'm currently collecting some of my better poems for an anthology to be published posthumously.'

'Oh good!' said the girl, with true feeling. 'I shall look forward to that.'

**812.** A friend of mine is a poet and he's almost starving. He says that rhyme doesn't pay.

**813.** The little old lady went to the post office and handed over the counter a large parcel, on which she'd written 'Fragile' numerous times and in large letters.

Counter clerk: Is there anything breakable in this parcel?

Little old lady: Of course not! 'Fragile' simply means 'unbreakable' in Latvian.

**814.** A scientist in Oxford has spent years trying to cross a pheasant with a guitar – he wants the pheasants to make music when they are plucked.

**815.** Did you hear about the Scotsman who died of a broken heart? He was tired of reading jokes about how mean the Scots are so he went into his nearest pub and ordered a round for everyone.

'That's very kind of you, sir,' commented the barman. 'There's almost 50 people in here. I didn't know you Jews were so generous.'

**816.** The Scotsman was visiting in London for the day and called upon a lady of pleasure in Soho and, after he had partaken of her bodily delights, he gave her £2,000.

'Why, that's incredibly generous of you!' exclaimed the surprised lady. 'No man has ever before given me so much. And yet, from your accent, you sound Scottish. Which part of Scotland do you come from?'

'From Edinburgh,' replied the Scotsman.

'How fantastic! My father works in Edinburgh.'

'I know,' said the Scotsman. 'When your father heard I was coming to London he asked me to bring you a share of his Lottery winnings – £2,000.'

**817.** The difference between a Scotsman and an Englishman can easily be discovered by letting loose a cow in their front gardens.

An Englishman will wail to his wife, 'Come quick and help me get rid of this horrible cow that's eating my prize lawn!'

The Scotsman will call to his wife, 'Come quick and bring a bucket – there's a cow on the lawn and it wants milking.'

**818.** The Englishman was in a restaurant in Scotland when he was suddenly attacked by a severe burst of coughing and sneezing – and he sneezed so violently that his false teeth flew out of his mouth and dropped to the floor, where they broke at the feet of a Scotsman.

'Don't worry, sir,' said the Scotsman. 'My brother will soon get you a new pair and at far less cost than an English dentist would charge. And he can provide a suitable set almost immediately.'

The Englishman couldn't believe his luck and gladly accepted the Scotsman's offer.

The Scotsman left the restaurant and returned ten minutes later with a pair of false teeth which he handed to the Englishman.

'Fantastic!' exclaimed the Englishman, trying the teeth. 'They fit perfectly. Your brother must be a very clever dentist.'

'Oh, he's not a dentist,' replied the Scotsman. 'He's an undertaker.'

**819.** 1st spy: I think Claude has become a mole.

2nd spy: How do you know?

1st spy: Because he's started eating worms and burying himself in the garden.

**820.** There I was, stranded in a strange town, and I urgently needed to use the public telephone.

Unfortunately, a rather plump lady was busily flipping through the pages of the phone book and so I could not get to the phone.

I waited patiently. Still the plump lady scanned the pages of the phone book.

After ten minutes, I grew a little exasperated (it's a small flower related to the tulip) and gently tapped the plump lady on the shoulder.

'Excuse me,' I said. 'Can I help you find a number in the phone book?'

'Oh,' she replied. 'I'm not exactly looking for a number. My daughter is expecting her first child next month and she's asked me to suggest some names for it. That's why I'm looking in the phone book – to see if I can find some nice-sounding names to suggest.'


**821.** Once I was out on a country walk in an area I'd never been to before. I enjoyed the beautiful scenery and soon I came to a stream – the other side of which was a country bakery from which came the delicious smell of fresh bread.

That stream was a bit too wide for me to jump across safely, but the water did not look too deep, although it was a bit muddy and I could not see the bottom.

A young girl was sitting by the side of the stream.

'Hello!' I said. 'Do you live near here?'

'Yes,' replied the girl.

'That's good,' I said. 'Then can you tell me how deep the stream is. Would I be able to walk across?'

'I think so,' replied the girl. 'The water isn't very deep.'

'Thanks,' I said, and stepped into the stream, only to sink into the water up to my neck.

'Hey!' I shouted to the girl, who was now giggling. 'I thought you said the water wasn't very deep.'

'I didn't know,' giggled the girl. 'I thought it was shallow. The water only manages to cover the legs of ducks and swans.'

**822.** Jake and his son Gabriel were farmers. From birth, they had lived in a small, remote village surrounded by mountains. Due to its location, television reception was impossible.

Jake and Gabriel had never even visited a town – let alone a major city. But all that was to change when they received a letter from a lawyer stating that they were the major beneficiaries under a distant relative's will. They were asked to attend a meeting with the lawyer in the city.

Jake and Gabriel were rather nervous about visiting a large, crowded city, but eventually they arrived at the multi-storey office block which housed the lawyer's firm.

As they waited in reception, Jake saw an elderly, very wrinkled woman press a button on one of the walls. Two metal doors slid open and the woman got in, pressed the number 21, and the doors closed.

A display panel above the doors showed numbers that started to count up to 21, then paused for a while before dropping rapidly. When the numbers stopped to be replaced by the letter G, the metal doors opened and a beautiful young woman walked out into the reception area.

'Did you see that?' Gabriel asked his son. 'We must bring your mother here. I wonder how much it would cost to put her in that contraption and make her look 21 so quickly.'

**823.** Reports are just coming in about a woman photographer in Clapham who committed suicide by drinking a bottle of varnish. She left a note saying she did it because she wanted a glossy finish.

**824.** On Wednesday, three rather naïve gangsters hi-jacked a submarine, and then demanded a million pounds – and three parachutes.

**825.** The reason why women have at least two good friends is because they need at least one to talk *to* and one or more to talk *about*.

**826.** Men are like a computer software package. Soon after you sign up to one a better model becomes available.

**827.** The only time she desires a man's company is when he owns one.

**828.** The reason that women generally have smaller feet than men is due to the evolutionary process. Smaller feet allow women to stand closer to the kitchen sink.

# POLITICS

**829.** What's a bore hole?
A politician's mouth.

**830.** What do you call an honest, intelligent politician?
Extinct.

**831.** Not all politicians should be shot – some should be guillotined.

**832.** Why does it take longer to build a snowman that looks like a politician than it does to build an ordinary snowman?
Because to be more realistic, you have to spend extra time hollowing out the head.

**833.** The danger with political jokes is that sometimes they get elected.

**834.** There is no such thing as a 'cheap politician' – they actually cost a fortune.

**835.** What do aliens and intelligent politicians have in common?

People talk about them but rarely see them – and some wonder if they exist at all.

**836.** The politician told his wife that he needed to get more headlines in order to advance his career. His wife said she thought he had enough lines on his forehead already.

**837.** The politician was on a fact-finding mission overseas and, when he arrived at the airport of one small country, he was greeted by a jostling crowd of newspaper reporters.

'Have you come to see the brothels?' asked one reporter.

The politician was temporarily stunned. Then, not wanting to offend, asked politely, 'Are there any brothels here?'

The next day there were banner headlines in the newspaper: VISITING POLITICIAN ASKS: 'ARE THERE ANY BROTHELS?'

**838.** Why is it that lunatics and criminals are not allowed to vote – but you *are* allowed to vote for *them*.

**839.** I understand that they are going to erect a huge statue in Trafalgar Square of .... [insert the name of your own least favourite politician]. They are doing it so the pigeons can express the views of us all.

**840.** Someone once said that politicians stand for whatever the people will fall for.


**841.** A relative of mine, Andrew, once went canvassing on behalf of the Labour Party.

The first door he knocked on was opened by a formidable-looking lady .with a piercing voice. Seeing Andrew's Labour rosette, the lady launched into a tirade of abuse about the Labour Party, its leaders, MPs and supporters. 'Utter trash, the lot of them!' she snorted. 'And their policies – if they can ever find them and follow them – stink. Absolute garbage!'

The lady was about to shut the door when Andrew said, rather meekly, 'Does that mean you won't be voting Labour?'


**842.** Did you hear about the Conservative MP who, when drunk, revealed such terrifying views to a journalist that he was dumped by his local party organization, ostracized by his former friends, and had to go and live in Australia?

He is now a far off terror Tory.


**843.** When a politician says he's 100 per cent behind you, he usually forgets to mention he's also holding a knife.


**844.** Soon after the terrorists kidnapped six politicians and fed them to the lions and tigers in a zoo, the terrorists were captured, tried and sentenced to a long term in jail – for cruelty to animals.

**845.** He's just bought a Prime Minister watch. It's got two faces.

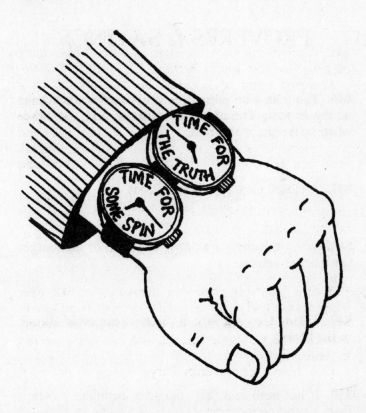

# PROVERBS & SAYINGS

**846.** The man who gives in and apologises when he is wrong is wise. The man who gives in and apologises when he is right is married.

**847.** A closed mouth gathers no foot.

**848.** When the chips are down – the fish or hamburger can't be far behind.

**849.** Taking the right fork in the road can avoid a knife in the back.

**850.** It has been said that change is inevitable – except from a vending machine.

**851.** The quickest way to find something is to buy a replacement for the thing you lost – then it will re-appear.

**852.** Never mention the number 288 in polite company – it's two gross.

**853.** A lack of curiosity kills the chat.

**854.** If at first you don't succeed – then you probably shouldn't try skydiving.

**855.** The more you understand, the less you realize you know.

**856.** Every woman worries about the future until she has acquired a husband, whereas men never worry about the future until they get a wife.

**857.** The less people know, the more stubbornly they know it.

**858.** The first sign of old age is when you still chase girls but can't remember why.

**859.** Men who call women 'birds' should remember that birds pick up worms.

# QUESTIONS

**860.** What do you get if you cross an insomniac, an agnostic and a dyslexic?

Someone who lies awake at night wondering if there is a dog.

**861.** When he was asked, 'What is the difference between ignorance and apathy?', he replied, 'I don't know – and I don't care!'

**862.** What is the best thing to take when you are run down?

The registration number of the vehicle.

**863.** If Santa Claus, an honest politician and a small boy are walking together along a street and simultaneously see a wallet on the ground, which of them picks up the wallet first?

The small boy. The other two don't really exist.

**864.** Where do horrible creatures like to eat?

At a beastro.

**865.** Where do you find the most fish?

Between the head and the tail.

**866.** What do you call a bee that doesn't speak clearly?
A mumble bee.

**867.** When the witch typed the manuscript of her book on her computer, which function on the computer did she like the most?
The spell checker.

**868.** What bone has no appeal to a dog?
A trombone.

**869.** What do you call a cat that likes eating lemons and drinking vinegar?
A sourpuss.

**870.** Why do bananas never snore?
Because they don't want to wake the rest of the bunch.

**871.** How can you easily pass a geometry test?
Know all the angles.

**872.** What is an American vampire's favourite holiday?
Fangsgiving.

**873.** What goes 'Buzz, zzub, buzz, zzub?'
A bee stuck to a yo-yo.

**874.** What steals bubbles from a bath?
A robber duck.

**875.** What do you get if you cross a clown with a pair of knickers?
Jester drawers.

**876.** How was business for the man who sold lions to zoos?
He was doing a roaring trade.

**877.** Where do private detectives do their shopping?
At a *snooper*market.

**878.** What do you call a man who steals a cut of meat from a butcher's shop?
A chop lifter.

**879.** What is small, furry, and used to chase outlaws in America?
A posse cat.

**880.** Why did the bees go on strike?
Because they wanted shorter flowers and more honey.

**881.** What happened when the computer fell on the floor?
It slipped a disk.

**882.** What famous detective liked bubble baths?
Sherlock Foams.

**883.** Why did the vampire's girlfriend tell him to use mouthwash?
Because he had bat breath.

**884.** Why was the baby cat playing with the bandages?
Because it wanted to be a first aid kit.

**885.** What has to be taken before you can get it?
A photograph.

**886.** What is at the back of a bee?
It's bee-hind.

**887.** What jackets can't you wear?
Jacket potatoes.

**888.** What does an Eskimo use to keep his house together?
Ig-glue.

**889.** What type of colourful bow is impossible to untie?
A rainbow.

**890.** Who can hold up trains without being arrested?
Bridesmaids and pageboys.


**891.** What was the name of the very first insect?
Adamant.


**892.** What do you get if you put your head in a bowl of an alcoholic fruit drink?
Punch up the nose.


**893.** What goes: 'Dot, dash, dot, dot, croak'?
A morse toad.


**894.** What is small, green, solves crimes and rubs its back legs together?
A grass copper.


**895.** What sort of novels do birds like to read?
Trillers.


**896.** After a visit to the cinema, what did the vampire ask his girlfriend?
Do you want to go somewhere for a bite?


**897.** What happened to the naughty witch at school?
She was ex-spelled.

**898.** What is red, sticky and bites people in the neck?
A *jam*pire.

**899.** What do you call twins who steal things?
A pair of nickers.

**900.** Why did the cat give birth in a rubbish bin?
Because it read the notice on the side of the bin:
'Place your litter here.'

**901.** What do you get if you cross a bee with a hand-bell?
A humdinger.

**902.** What do you call a hippo that jumps around on one leg?
A hoppo.

**903.** What do you call an exploding sheep?
Baa-boom!

**904.** What do female sheep wear in school?
Ewe-niforms.

**905.** What can you hold without touching it?
A conversation.

**906.** What's it like to be kissed by a vampire?
It's a pain in the neck.


**907.** What is black and white and bounces up and down?
A penguin on a pogo stick.


**908.** What is furry, white and smells of peppermint?
A polo bear.


**909.** What do you call a very small person who likes travelling on the Paris underground while making a constant beat?
A Metro-gnome.


**910.** Why was the spider ill?
Because it caught a nasty bug.


**911.** Why did everyone in the courtroom keep jumping up and down?
Because it was a kangaroo court.


**912.** What do you call a Japanese piano that keeps telling jokes?
A Yamaha-ha.


**913.** What goes 'quack, quack, boom'?
A duck in a mine field.

**914.** What flies but doesn't go anywhere when it's up?
A flag.


**915.** What is the most use when it is used up?
An umbrella.


**916.** What is it when a bike suddenly starts to bite people?
The start of a vicious cycle.


**917.** You break it when you say it. What is it?
Silence.


**918.** What is black and white, has a beak, likes fish and is very noisy?
A penguin with a drum kit.


**919.** What did one eye say to the other eye?
'Between you and me, something smells.'


**920.** How do male students sort their clothes?
Into three piles: might be clean, dirty but wearable, and dirty and smelly.


**921.** What do you get if you cross a chicken with a clock?
An alarm cluck.

**922.** What do you call a plump pet cat that has eaten a duck?

A duck-filled fatty puss.

**923.** How can you stop milk from turning sour?

Leave it in the cow.

**924.** What tuba cannot be played?

A tuba toothpaste.

**925.** What walks about saying, 'Ouch, ouch, ouch, ouch, ouch, ouch, ouch, ouch'?

An octopus wearing shoes that are too tight.

**926.** Who was old, had a lot of children, and was rather sticky?

The Old Woman Who Lived In the Glue.

**927.** What did the skunk do in church?

It sat in a phew.

**928.** What is small, round, smells and giggles?

A tickled onion.

**929.** What says 'Oom, oom'?

A backward cow.

**930.** What game do mice like to play?
Hide and squeak.

**931.** What is the difference between a coyote and a flea?
One howls on the prairie, while the other prowls on the hairy.

**932.** What do you get if you cross a pig with an evergreen tree that has cones?
A porker-pine.

**933.** Why was the young glow worm a bit sad?
Because it had glowing pains.

**934.** What game do horses like to play?
Stable tennis.

**935.** What do you use for measuring the noise a dog makes?
A barking meter.

**936.** Why did the baby pig eat so much food?
So it could make a hog of itself.

**937.** What was the largest moth in the world?
A mam-moth.

**938.** Where do cows go for outings?
To the moo-vies.

**939.** Where do intelligent cows like to visit on their holidays?
Moo-seums.

**940.** Where do very young fish go to be educated?
Plaice school.

**941.** What do young witches like best in school?
Spelling lessons.

**942.** What do you get if a witch gets flu?
Cold spells.

**943.** What is the difference between an oak tree and a very tight shoe?
One makes acorns – the other makes corns ache.

**944.** What slithers along the ground and works for the Government?
A civil serpent.

**945.** What ring can never be round?
A boxing ring.

**946.** Where did the major-general keep his armies?
Up his sleevies.

**947.** What game do cows play at parties?
Moo-sical chairs.

**948.** Why do storks only lift one leg?
Because if they lifted the other leg, they would fall over.

**949.** Where does Friday come before Tuesday?
In a dictionary.

**950.** What are the largest ants in the world?
Gi-ants and eleph-ants.

**951.** Where do underwater creatures go when their teeth hurt?
To a dental sturgeon.

**952.** What is very big and says, 'Fum, Fo, Fi, Fee?'
A backward giant.

**953.** How did the otters manage to travel at 50 miles per hour on the motorway?
By travelling in an otter-mobile.

**954.** Why are rivers lazy?
Because they seldom leave their beds.


**955.** Which side of a sheep has the most wool?
The outside.


**956.** How can you easily make a witch itch?
Remove the 'w'.


**957.** How do you stop toadstools appearing in your garden?
Give the toads some sofas instead.


**958.** What fish races through the water at 90 miles an hour?
A motor pike.


**959.** Why did the singer gargle with soup?
Because she was a souprano.


**960.** What tiles are the most difficult to fix to the bathroom wall?
Reptiles.


**961.** What happens to plants left in the maths teacher's room?
They grow square roots.

**962.** How do you start a flea race?
One, two, flea, go!

**963.** What is in Paris, is very tall and wobbles?
The Trifle Tower.

**964.** What did the vampire doctor shout out in his waiting room?
'Necks please!'

**965.** What do you call a witch's husband when he's travelling on her broomstick?
A flying sorcerer.

**966.** What do police officers eat for tea?
Truncheon meat.

**967.** What is the favourite flower of a pet frog?
A croakus.

**968.** What two letters of the alphabet hurt teeth?
D. K.

**969.** What do elves and pixies have to do when they come home from school?
Gnomework.

**970.** What clothes does a house wear?
A dress.


**971.** What do you call a lot of girls waiting in line to buy some dolls with yellow-blonde hair?
A Barbie-queue.


**972.** What carries a basket, goes through the woods, visits grandma and steals money?
Little Red Robin Hood.


**973.** If rocket scientists are all so clever, why can they only count backwards, 10, 9, 8, 7 . . . ?


**974.** Why is it that bills seem to travel through the postal system at a much faster speed than cheques?

# RELATIONSHIPS &
# ROMANCE

**975.** Last night he met a woman in a bar. He chatted to her and soon they were kissing and cuddling. Then they went outside and walked towards her car where their passion increased. She took out her car key, kissed him passionately and told him: 'You can have anything you want.' So he took the key and her car.

**976.** The man in the nightclub was trying to get a girl interested in him and was patting her knee and almost begging her to go for a walk outside in the moonlight. The girl looked at him and said, 'You remind me of a boxer.'

'That's great,' said the man, thinking he had charmed the girl. 'Which one – a younger version of Ali?'

'No,' replied the girl, 'my Father's dog, Rover.'

**977.** Jeremy was at a drinks party and went up to a pretty young woman who was standing in the corner of the room. 'You know,' he said, 'you're so attractive that I would go to the end of the world for you.'

'That's good,' said the young woman. 'Please stay there.'

**978.** After going out on a date with Gareth she said that she found him so conceited it was a night of a thousand I's.

**979.** He's just found the perfect girl to take to the dance – he's got two left feet and she's got two right feet.

**980.** I recently joined a dating agency and said I wanted to meet someone small and cute and who liked climbing and the outdoor life. It would also be good if her favourite foods were similar to mine: nuts and fruit. They matched me up with a squirrel.

**981.** When someone told me they had seen a beautiful woman on Jeremy's arm I said, 'He's never showed me that tattoo.'

**982.** The reason it is so difficult for women to find men who are good looking, sensitive and caring is because such men already have boyfriends.

**983.** When Jeremy eventually managed to get a girl to go out with him he took her to an expensive restaurant and, to impress her, ordered the whole meal in French. The girl and the waiter were amazed by this – especially as the restaurant was Chinese.

**984.** I recently went out with a feminist and when I heard a plane overhead I looked up and said, 'That's the mail plane.' She stamped her feet and said, 'It's so high up, how can you possibly tell what sex it is?'

**985.** She was so excited. At the weekend a handsome young man took her up the aisle . . . and showed her to her seat in the cinema.

**986.** When her boyfriend asked her how she got such shapely eyebrows she said, 'It takes a lot of pluck.'

**987.** My girlfriend and I have just broken up. It was all due to astrological circumstances. She was a water sign and I'm an earth sign, so our relationship soon turned to mud.

**988.** One of my friends has just broken off his relationship with a young woman. I was rather surprised as he had been going out with her for six months and they seemed very happy together. But my friend explained the reason for the break-up. He said she had suddenly started using 'dreadful four-letter words' – like 'ring', 'baby' ...

**989.** If you want to love your neighbour then it's best to make sure their spouse is away when you do it.

**990.** What words do you most fear hearing when you're making love to a woman?
  'Honey, I'm home.'

**991.** My boyfriend is a kung-fu expert. Last night he hit an insect on his side and broke one of his own ribs.

**992.** On my first date with my boyfriend I asked him if I could hold his hand, and he said, 'I can manage, thank you. It isn't very heavy.'

**993.** My boyfriend has a good head for money – it's got a little slot in the top . . .

**994.** I wouldn't say my boyfriend was stupid, but when we went to the park last night and I said I saw a poor, dead bird, he asked 'Where?' and looked up at the sky.

**995.** Most of my sister's boyfriends are like eggs – fresh, rotten or hard-boiled.

**996.** When my friend Albert discovered that his girlfriend was being unfaithful to him he asked her, 'Why do you need another lover? Have you had enough of me?'

'Darling,' replied his girlfriend, 'it's because I *haven't* had enough of you that I need a lover.'

**997.** My boyfriend was told about the birds and bees very early in life. Shortly afterwards he was stung by a bee – and was extremely worried for the next nine months.

**998.** Somehow, I don't think I'm going to marry my current boyfriend. Last night when I casually asked him how much money he had in the bank, he said he would have to go home and open the pig to find out.

**999.** I tried computer dating once – but it was a bit disappointing. When I took it to dinner and then a disco, the computer didn't have much to say.

**1000.** Young man: Darling, I dreamt about you last night.

Pretty young girl: Did you?

Young man: No – you wouldn't let me!

**1001.** My new girlfriend is like a grapefruit. Whenever I squeeze her, she spits at me.

**1002.** 'I thought you said your new girlfriend was a model? With the greatest of respect, she doesn't really look like one. What does she model?'
  'Halloween masks.'

**1003.** My girlfriend is a real sex object. Whenever I mention sex, she objects.

**1004.** My girlfriend says she only weighs eight stones – but I reckon the stones must be the size of boulders.

**1005.** My girlfriend can never understand why her brother has five sisters and she only has four.

**1006.** When someone asked my girlfriend if she ever had much trouble making up her mind, she said, 'I'm not sure. Maybe yes. Maybe no.'

**1007.** This morning I bought my girlfriend a sexy new nightdress. Tonight I'll try to talk her out of it.

**1008.** My girlfriend speaks Italian like a native – a native from Scunthorpe.

**1009.** I'll never forget my first girlfriend. It was real puppy love. Every time I went to kiss her, she said 'Woof!'

**1010.** Yesterday I had lunch with an old friend. She was in tears.

'What's wrong?' I asked.

'It's George,' she replied. 'He invested a lot of money on the stock market and lost it. To try to recoup his losses he took out huge loans on his house and borrowed money from relatives – and then put it all in a company he thought would do well. It was a wild speculation. He's just told me that the firm he invested in has filed for bankruptcy – so he's lost everything.'

'Oh dear,' I said. 'And I thought things were going so well for you both. You must be very worried. Weren't you planning to get married this summer?'

'Yes,' she replied. 'Now I wonder what George will do without me.'

**1011.** I've just come out of hospital. I was in there for six weeks as a result of my boyfriend throwing me over. He caught me out with another man and threw me over a cliff.

**1012.** My boyfriend takes me to all the best nightclubs – maybe one day they'll let us in.

**1013.** When Harry told his girlfriend he was seeing a psychiatrist, she admitted that she was seeing her boss, the local garage mechanic and a rather handsome window cleaner.

**1014.** Bill can read his girlfriend like a book – in bed.

**1015.** Paul: Is it true that you proposed to that awful Gruntswick woman at the party last night?

David: Unfortunately, yes.

Paul: And she accepted your proposal. But didn't you only meet her at the party?

David: Yes. But after five or six dances together I couldn't think of anything else to talk about.

**1016.** When I told my cousin that I'd fixed him up with a date with an attractive librarian, he said, 'What part of Libraria does she come from?'

**1017.** Catherine snuggled up to her boyfriend, Robert, and whispered, 'Darling, now that you want us to get engaged, will you give me a ring?'

Robert smiled lovingly at Catherine and replied, 'Certainly! What's your phone number?'


**1018.** A friend of mine recently introduced me to his new girlfriend and said he was madly in love with her and was going to marry her in a few days' time.

I recognized her as the notorious woman who had slept with half the men in Basingstoke. I managed to get my friend into a quiet corner and broke this news to him. But he just shrugged his shoulders and said, 'So? Basingstoke's not very big.'


**1019.** My friend, Freda, has been writing to a male penfriend for eighteen months. He lives 200 miles away.

Gradually their letters grew more and more romantic, until eventually they felt they had to meet each other.

'Unfortunately,' wrote the man, 'I am seven feet tall, have an enormous nose, and my ears stick out.'

'Don't worry,' wrote back Freda. 'Your letters showed me your true self. But when you arrive at Paddington Station, please hold a carnation in your left hand so that I can recognize you.'


**1020.** In romance, opposites frequently attract. That is why poor young girls are often attracted to rich old men.


**1021.** I recently overhead two women talking on a train. One said to the other, 'I hear you've broken up with John. But only last week you told me it was love at first sight.'

'I know,' came the reply, 'it *was* love at first sight. But when I saw him for the second time I went off him.'

**1022.** My first job was as a clerical officer and I really fancied a young typist. Eventually I plucked up enough courage and asked her, 'Could I have a date?'

'Certainly,' she replied. 'How about 1066?'


**1023.** 'It's not fair! I've proposed to two boyfriends without avail.'

'Maybe next time you should wear a veil?'


**1024.** 'Where have I seen your beautiful face before?'

'I don't know – it's always been between my ears.'


**1025.** 'I love you much, much more than anyone else in the whole wide world.'

'You mean, you've had them all, too?'


**1026.** Young girl: Darling, will you love me when I get old?

Young man: Of course I'll love you. Our love will grow stronger with each passing hour. Our love will endure throughout eternity. But you won't be looking like your mother, will you?


**1027.** Samantha said to her sister, 'My boyfriend has finally persuaded me to say "yes" '.

'Fantastic!' replied Katie. 'Congratulations. When will the wedding be?

'Wedding? Who said anything about a wedding?'

**1028.** Emily: Dearest, will you still love me when my hair has all gone grey?

Richard: Of course, dear. If I loved you when your hair was blonde then brunette then black then red – why should grey made any difference?

**1029.** 'I'll give you just fifteen minutes to stop doing that ...'

**1030.** When I first went out with my girlfriend, she made me lay all my cards on the table – Barclaycard, American Express ...

**1031.** The beautiful young girl was walking along the street when a young man walked up beside her and said, 'Hello, beautiful! Haven't we met somewhere before?'

The girl gave him a frosty stare and continued walking.

'Huh!' snorted the young man. 'Now I realize my mistake – I thought you were my mother.'

'That's impossible,' retorted the girl. 'I'm married.'

**1032.** 'That man's annoying me.'

'Why? He's not even looking at you.'

'I know. *That's* what's annoying me!'

**1033.** Mavis fell in love with her boyfriend at second sight – the first time she didn't know he had any money.

**1034.** It had been a very enjoyable party and Jake, a young man with a Texan drawl, appeared to get on very well with a pretty young English girl named Sally – although both had met each other for the first time at the party.

'Can I see you home?' inquired Jake.

Sally reached into her handbag and produced a photograph of her house.


**1035.** Peter received the following letter from his girl-friend:

Darling Peter,

I'm so sorry I quarrelled with you and called off our wedding. I'm terribly, terribly sorry for all the hateful and spiteful things I said about you and do hope you will forgive me. Whatever you want of me I shall try to give – and do hope you will give me one more chance. I know I said I was leaving you for Tony, saying he was a much better man than you, but I never honestly meant it. Tony means nothing to me. You are the only one in my heart. You, Peter, are all that I desire. Please forgive me and take me back,

Your ever-loving Janice.

PS May I take this opportunity to congratulate you on winning such a large amount on the Lottery.


**1036.** The young girl was snuggling up to the young man on the sofa and said, 'Would you like to see my birthmark?'

'Yes,' replied the young man. 'How long have you had it?'


**1037.** Sally and Jane were talking about the wonderful party they had just attended.

'That George was really hunky,' said Sally.

'I know,' sighed Jane.

'He and I got on really well,' said Sally. 'He wants to see me again and asked for my phone number.'

'Did you give it to him?' asked Jane.

'I told him my number was in the phone book.'

'Does he know your surname?' asked Jane.

'I told him that was in the phone book, too. I can't wait until he rings ...'

**1038.** Some young women are music lovers – and others can do it without.

**1039.** 'Will you kiss me?'
'But I have scruples.'
'That's all right. I've been vaccinated.'

**1040.** Young girl: Darling, do you think I should wear my short green Chinese silk dress or my long fawn woollen dress tonight?

Young man: I don't mind what you wear, dearest. You know I'll love you through thick or thin.

**1041.** 'How was your first date with John?'
'Oh, it was all right until after dinner. But on the way home he stopped the car in a lonely lane and started kissing me and generally distracting my attention. He then started feeling my bra and around my panties – but I fooled him. I'd hidden my money in my shoe ...'

**1042.** My girlfriend told me last night that she really loved me. But I think it's only puppy love as she was panting, licking my face, and rubbing me behind the ears at the time.

**1043.** Adrian: Why do all the men find Victoria so attractive?

Simon: Because of her speech impediment.

Adrian: Her speech impediment?

Simon: Yes. She can't say 'no'.

**1044.** Cuthbert: Darling, if we get married do you think you will be able to live on my income?

Ethel: Of course, darling. But what are *you* going to live on?

**1045.** 'Sir, I'd very much like to marry your daughter,' said young Wilkins, a junior clerk in the company in which his prospective bride's father was the Personnel Officer.
'I see,' replied the man. 'Write out your qualifications, name, address and any other details you think appropriate and leave it with me. If no other suitable applicants turn up, then I'll ask you to come for a further interview.'

**1046.** Mabel and Arthur had been living together for 45 years as man and wife.

One day Mabel was reading a romantic women's magazine when she suddenly looked up at Arthur and said, 'Why don't we get married?'

'Don't be crazy,' replied Arthur. 'Who would want to marry us at our time of life?'

**1047.** Overheard in a dimly lit nightclub: 'Do you know the difference between sex and conversation?'

'No.'

'Then why not come back to my apartment and lie down while I talk to you?'

**1048.** With so many romantics, they must be on Crowd Nine.

**1049.** 'Would you agree to come out with me tonight?'

'I'm sorry, but I never go out with perfect strangers.'

'Who said I was perfect?'

**1050.** 'And how is your son?' asked Mrs Goldberg.

'Oh, he is a constant joy to me,' replied Mrs Cohen.

'But how is that possible? Surely you know he is homosexual?'

'Yes, I know', said Mrs Cohen, 'but recently he has been going out with such a nice Jewish lawyer.'

**1051.** When the cannibal girl was 21 her mother said, 'I think it's time you found yourself a nice edible young bachelor.'

**1052.** My first kiss was rather romantic. I was 11 at the time and had braces to help straighten my teeth. My girlfriend wore braces on her teeth too – and it took the fire brigade half an hour to unhook us.

**1053.** Claudia refuses to go out with married men – she insists they come in to her flat!

**1054.** 'Oh, Brian, Mum wouldn't like it.'
   'Your mother isn't going to get it!'

**1055.** Pretty young girl: What are we going to do today?

Young man: How about a drive in the country?

Pretty young girl: Will there be any kissing and cuddling and parking in lonely lanes and all that sort of thing?

Young man: Certainly not!

Pretty young girl: Then what are we going for?

**1056.** Young man to attractive young girl: I'd like to see you in a two-piece outfit – slippers!

**1057.** The nurse ended her romance with William because she felt she had been deceived.
   William had told her that they had a lot in common as he frequently had to deal with poor hearts and livers. She thought he was a doctor – now she's found out he works in a butcher's shop.

**1058.** 'I saw you! I saw what you got up to last night!' said little Emily when her big sister's boyfriend came to visit.

'Oh!' said the boy, blushing. 'If you don't tell your parents I'll give you £5.'

'That's very generous,' replied Emily. 'All the others only offered me £1.'

**1059.** Greg had asked if he could marry Mr Brown's daughter.

'Would you still love her as much if she was poor?' asked Mr Brown, who was a self-made multi-millionaire.

'Of course, sir!' replied Greg, with feeling.

'Then I'm not happy about you marrying her,' replied Mr Brown. 'I don't want a fool in the family.'

**1060.** Fred is extremely broadminded – he's got nothing else on his mind.

**1061.** Young man: Oh, my gorgeous, sweetest darling! Am I the first man you've ever been to bed with?

Young girl: Of course you are! Why do all you men always ask the same stupid question?

**1062.** A couple I know were having trouble with their love life so they went to seek professional help.

They were advised to put more variety into their sex lives – so now he tries to juggle and she does magic tricks while they make love.

**1063.** A friend of mine was in New York and was approached by a prostitute.

'Would you like a good time?' asked the woman.

'How much?' asked my friend.

'What do you think I'm worth?' asked the prostitute.

'$50?' suggested my friend.

'Cheapskate!' snapped the prostitute. 'You only get ugly trash for that sort of money!'

Later that evening my friend was with his wife, waiting for a taxi outside the hotel. The prostitute happened to walk by and, as she did so, she hissed, 'See! I told you $50 would only get you ugly trash!'

**1064.** I was in a chemist's shop this morning and a very nervous young man came in and asked for a packet of anti-sickness pills and a packet of contraceptives.

The shop assistant looked at the trembling young man, smiled and said, 'If it makes you sick, why do it?'

**1065.** The only reason Keith's wife says he is good in bed is because she is very houseproud and when he makes love he doesn't disturb the sheets and blankets.

**1066.** Although she was only the architect's daughter, she let the borough surveyor.

**1067.** He thinks the best shape for a woman is to have a narrow waist and a broad mind.

**1068.** The university lecturer was speaking to an audience of townspeople. He was attempting to prove there was a definite connection between happiness and the amount of sex in people's lives.

To help prove his point, he asked those in the audience who indulged every night to raise their hands. Only 5 per cent did so, all laughing merrily.

He then asked how many indulged about once a week, and 70 per cent raised their hands, smiling contentedly as they did so.

Then the people who indulged once every month were asked to raise their hands, but it was noticeable that these people neither laughed or smiled.

The lecturer felt that this proved his point – but to show how obvious this matter was, he asked those who only indulged once every year to raise their hands. A tall man at the back of the hall leapt from his chair, waving his hand and laughing loudly.

The lecturer was astonished at this apparent contradiction to his lecture, and he asked the man if he could explain why he was so happy.

The man replied, 'Certainly. It's tonight! It's tonight!'

**1069.** I've got the most sexy, witty, creative, intelligent wife in the world . . . I just hope her husband doesn't know about it.

**1070.** Brian had great problems finding a woman. Indeed, he found it difficult to get *anyone* to like him as he was very ugly and had an irritating horse-like laugh which he appended to the end of almost every sentence.

Then one day he slipped on an icy pavement and was taken to hospital to be X-rayed for a suspected broken leg and wrist.

It was then that it happened. As the X-rays were being taken, his eyes met those of the radiographer and they fell in love – she knew what was in him.

**1071.** 'Is it true you've fallen in love with Dracula?'
'Yes. It was love at first bite.'
'My! How fangtastic.'

# RELIGION

**1072.** Adam in the Garden of Eden was getting rather bored talking to the plants and animals. 'Couldn't I have another human to talk to?' he asked God.

'Well,' said God, 'I could create a woman.'

'What's that?' asked Adam.

'It's human, rather like a man, but she can pleasure you in many ways. She can cook, clean, look after your every need and do whatever you want her to do. She will never argue or nag. With a woman you can have incredible sex whenever and however you want. But in order to create such a woman I will need to take two of your ribs, two toes and two fingers.'

'Oh!' said Adam. 'That seems rather a lot. What would I get for just one rib?'

**1073.** What time was Adam created?
A little before Eve.

**1074.** One of the advantages of being Adam, the first man in the world, is that he didn't have to listen to Eve wail on about all the men she could have married.

**1075.** It's quite obvious that Adam was an idiot. There he was, in paradise, with a beautiful, naked woman and what does he want to do? Kiss and cuddle? Make love? No – he wants to eat fruit!

**1076.** The main attraction to him of atheism is that it's non-prophet making.

**1077.** An atheist was in a small boat off the coast of Australia when the weather suddenly turned stormy and violent waves threw him into the water.

As he began swimming he saw a large shark heading towards him, so he called for God to help him. But God replied: 'How can I help you if you don't believe?'

'OK' replied the atheist. 'Then at least make the shark believe in you.'

When the shark was only a short distance from the atheist he heard the shark say 'Dear God,' and the atheist sighed with relief. The shark continued: 'Thank you for the man/food we are about to receive …'

**1078.** The writer of television soap operas had grown very old, so he went to see the vicar of his local church to discuss funeral arrangements and to declare his firm belief in reincarnation. After much persuasion, and a large donation to church funds, the vicar agreed that the writer's tombstone could be inscribed: 'To be continued …'

**1079.** One tribe of cannibals was converted by missionaries to becoming good Catholics – they ate fishermen only on Fridays.

**1080.** One angel's hobby was compiling a list of people's last words. His favourites included: 'Pull the pin out and count to *what*?', 'Which wire was I supposed to cut?' and 'There's no need to worry. These are the types of wild mushrooms it's perfectly safe to eat.'

**1081.** How can a priest keep fit?
Exorcise regularly.

**1082.** There I was in the desert, walking about all alone. Then I heard a voice saying: 'Yea, though I walk through the valley of the shadow of death, I will fear no evil.'

I looked around. No one. Not even a camel.

The voice continued: 'For thou art with me, thy rod and thy staff they comfort me.'

Then I realised the voice was coming from a tree near a small oasis. It was a psalm tree.

**1083.** What did John The Baptist and Winnie The Pooh have in common?
Their middle names.

**1084.** I can't understand those people who say they have just found God – I didn't know He was lost.

**1085.** The only times a lot of people go to church is when they go to see things thrown: water at christenings, confetti and rice at weddings, and earth at funerals.

**1086.** Just outside the church, the small boy found a £1 coin and picked it up.

The vicar saw the boy and said, 'Hello! I see you've found a coin. Are you going to keep it?'

'No, sir,' replied the boy.

'Excellent, excellent!' beamed the vicar.

'I'm going to spend it,' said the boy.

**1087.** A mohel opened a shop and displayed some plastic dustbins in the window. (A mohel is the person who carries out the Jewish circumcision operation.)

Anyway, a man went into the shop and said, 'I'd like a plastic dustbin, please.'

The mohel replied, 'I'm afraid I don't sell them.'

'But you've got plastic dustbins in the window!' exclaimed the man.

'So?' shrugged the mohel, 'what would you have put in the window?'

**1088.** Cynthia: What do you think of the new clergyman?

Janice: Very good. I didn't know much about sin until he came.

**1089.** The vicar asked the young man, 'Are you ever troubled by erotic thoughts about the opposite sex?'

'No,' replied the young man, 'I rather like the thoughts. They're no trouble.'

**1090.** If Moses had been a lawyer, there wouldn't have been Ten Commandments. Instead there would have been many thousands of commandments, each with numerous clauses and sub-clauses.

**1091.** Jewish men are very optimistic. The proof of this is that they all have a bit cut off before they know how long it's going to be.

**1092.** Less than half a per cent of dead bagpipe players go to Heaven. That's because if any more went, it would be Hell.

# SHOPS & SERVICES

**1093.** Whenever he goes out with his wife he holds her hand. That way he hopes to be able to steer her away from expensive shops.

**1094.** The student was trying to save money in order to go on a foreign holiday so she got a Saturday job in a local chemist's shop. On her first day at work a man came in wanting to buy a thermometer. 'What one would you recommend?' asked the customer.

The girl picked up several boxes of thermometers, looked at them and said, 'Well, I know people think German products are reliable so I suggest you get the Fahrenheit one.'

**1095.** A woman went into a hardware shop and asked the assistant if he had long nails.

'Certainly!' he replied. 'But don't ask me to scratch your back with them. I've heard that tired old joke too many times.'

'I wasn't going to tell a joke,' said the woman. 'Of course I want to buy real nails, not fingernails. Can I buy some?'

'Certainly, madam,' replied the assistant. 'How long do you want them?'

The woman sighed and replied, 'At least a few years. They're to repair the kids' rabbit hutch.'

**1096.** 'Do you sell dogs' meat?'

'Certainly – if they come here with their owner.'


**1097.** People in Britain are becoming much stronger. Forty years ago it would take two men to carry £20 of supermarket shopping. Now, even a small child can carry it.


**1098.** I went to the perfume counter in a department store and asked to see and smell some different types of perfume. The assistant asked me, 'Is the perfume for your wife, sir – or would you like to see something more expensive?'


**1099.** Business in some London shops is now so slow that when I picked up a bracelet in a jewellery shop and asked the young lady manager, 'Would you take anything off for cash?', she replied, 'For £100 you can see me topless. For £200 I'll take everything off.'


**1100.** Customer: I want a pen that writes underwater.

Shop assistant: Wouldn't you like it to write other words, too?'


**1101.** My wife is so stupid she went window shopping the other day – and came home with five windows.

**1102.** Yesterday I went shopping with my girlfriend and she went into the chemist's shop and asked if they had any mirrors.

'Do you want a hand mirror?' asked the sales assistant.

'No,' replied my girlfriend, 'I don't want to look at my hands in it. I want one I can see my face in.'


**1103.** He bought a piece of antique furniture quite cheaply from a seafood restaurant. It was Fish and Chippendale.


**1104.** Retired Army Colonel: I'd like some pepper, my good man.

Shop assistant: Certainly, sir! What sort would you like – white or black pepper?

Retired Army Colonel: Neither. I want toilet pepper!


**1105.** I wouldn't say my sister is stupid, but the other day she went into a petshop and bought some birdseed. She thinks that if she plants it, she'll grow a bird.


**1106.** After searching all over the department store's furnishing section, a woman sighed, 'They don't make antiques like they used to!'


**1107.** 'Is this a second-hand shop?'
'Yes.'
'Please can you fit one on my alarm clock?'

# SHORTIES

**1108.** The reason that God created Man before he created Woman is because He wanted a rough draft before He made perfection.

**1109.** Am I ambivalent? Well, yes and no.

**1110.** People say the world is full of apathy – but so what?

**1111.** A calendar is something that goes in one year and out the other.

**1112.** I wish people with closed minds wouldn't open their mouths so often.

**1113.** I once bought a house in the country. By the time I finished paying for it, it was in town.

**1114.** She says that it is impossible for men to get mad cow disease as all men are pigs.

**1115.** What is the difference between government bonds and men?

Bonds mature.

**1116.** After years of careful study, women have concluded that the easiest time to change a male is when he's a baby.

**1117.** He wanted to be a household name – so he changed his name to Hoover.

**1118.** He asked if he could call her later. She said she'd prefer it if he called her Caroline.

**1119.** He can only remember the names of people less than five feet two inches tall – he has a short memory.

**1120.** When he was born something really dreadful happened.

He survived.

**1121.** He's a well-balanced person. He has a chip on both shoulders.

**1122.** The two worst things about him are his face.

**1123.** He's got a good head on his shoulders – it's just a pity it's not on his neck.

**1124.** He recently took an intelligence test. The results came back negative.

**1125.** He's got something that makes women go crazy. Rabies.

**1126.** If you want to see something really funny, then look in a mirror.

**1127.** I wouldn't say she has a big mouth – but she puts her lipstick on with a paint-roller.

**1128.** His problem is that he stopped to think – but then forgot to re-start.

**1129.** People say there's safety in numbers. Quite right. A million lemmings can't possibly be wrong.

**1130.** If you don't stop telling jokes about my shortness of height I'll bite you in the knees.

**1131.** The length of a minute depends on whether you are the one doing the waiting, or are the one for whom other people are waiting.

**1132.** Whenever we have an electricity blackout it's then I discover that every torch in the house is just a useful container for storing dead batteries.

**1133.** Wars do not decide who is right ... they determine who is left.

**1134.** My young cousin thinks that a granary is a home for grandmothers.

**1135.** He thinks that a teetotaller is someone who keeps the score during a game of golf.

**1136.** He'd give his right arm to be ambidextrous.

**1137.** A bargain is something you buy that is cheaper than something you really want or need.

**1138.** When I was younger, I used to love Carol singing. Now I'm older, I love Carol sighing.

**1139.** I dream in colour – but it may be a pigment of my imagination.

**1140.** 'I've heard that you are an excellent fortune teller. Can you predict the next few months?'
'Certainly! December, January, February.'

**1141.** I once knew a man who thought he was a goat. He'd believed that ever since he was a young kid.

**1142.** Charles used to wear a pork pie hat, but he got fed up with the gravy running down his neck.

**1143.** I used to live in a house in Llanfihangel-Tay-y-llyn in Wales – but I had to move because I couldn't spell the address.

**1144.** He's so wealthy that he even bought a kid for his dog to play with.

**1145.** On the business front, sales of tiaras increased enormously this afternoon – it was tiara boom today!

**1146.** Five people broke out of prison last night by stealing a lorry load of sennapods. It is believed the criminals are still on the run.

**1147.** I always read the obituary columns every morning to see if I'm alive or dead.

**1148.** My wife reads the obituary columns and thinks it very odd that people keep dying in alphabetical order.

**1149.** Whenever I go to fancy dress parties, I always go as Napoleon. That way, I can keep one hand on my wallet.

**1150.** When you look just like your passport photo you know you're really too sick to travel.

**1151.** 'We hope the author will soon be needing our services.' *The Coffin Makers' Gazette.*

**1152.** 'The writer of this book is a genius. By the way, I must thank him for such a fantastic weekend at his cottage in the country. This, of course, in no way influenced my opinion of his work.' *A Female Critic.*

**1153.** 'This book is brilliant.' *Daily Liar.*

**1154.** 'He is a man who recognises true genius (he gave my novel a good review) and his latest book is excellent.' *A Back-scratcher.*

**1155.** 'He is certainly one of our best writers and will surely become as famous as William Shakespeare – the William Shakespeare of 112 Railway Arches, Neasden, Alaska.' *Anony Mouse.*

**1156.** I'm very sleepy. I had to get up at the crack of yawn.

**1157.** Last night I slept like a baby – I kept waking up and crying.

**1158.** Last night I dreamt I was eating my pillow, so when I woke up I felt a bit down in the mouth.

**1159.** Over the phone some voices are very difficult to extinguish.

**1160.** It's easy to make time fly: just throw an alarm clock over your shoulder.

**1161.** In the old days of the USSR, all the history books used to have loose leaves.

**1162.** Winter is the time when it is too cold to do all the boring things that it was too hot or too wet to do in Summer.

**1163.** I always know when Winter has arrived because that is when my neighbour returns my lawnmower.

**1164.** He started out in life with nothing. He still has most of it.

**1165.** She used to have a handle on life – but it broke.

# SONGS FOR FISH & ANIMALS

**1166.** 'Mackerel The Knife.'

**1167.** 'My Bear Lady.'

**1168.** 'I've Got Ewe Under My Skin.'

**1169.** 'Snake, Rattle And Mole.'

**1170.** 'Weasel Overcome.'

**1171.** 'Tie A Yellow Gibbon Round An Old Oak Tree.'

**1172.** 'Whale Meet Again.'

**1173.** 'Jack The Kipper'

**1174.** 'I'm Gonna Wash That Man Right Out Of My Bear.'

**1175.** 'Hit The Road Yak.'

**1176.** 'If You Were The Only Gill In The World.'

**1177.** 'Red Snails In The Sunset.'

**1178.** 'Amazing Plaice.'

**1179.** 'Salmon Chanted Evening.'

**1180.** 'Fly Me To Baboon.'

**1181.** 'Mullet Of Kintyre.'

**1182.** 'Long And Winding Toad.'

# SPEECHES & SPEAKING

**1183.** If I'm heckled during a speech one useful put down is to say to the heckler: 'You can go home now, your cage has been cleaned.'

**1184.** His speeches are so boring he puts more people to sleep than an anaesthetist.

**1185.** I have a slight impediment in my speech – my lawyer won't allow me to say anything.

**1186.** He's a man of few words – it's a great pity he repeats them for hours.

**1187.** He can talk in public for hours without a note – and usually without a point.

**1188.** A toastmaster is the person who starts the bull rolling.

**1189.** He is well-known for his boring speeches. But as he is chairman of a large company he is sometimes asked to speak at business dinners and conferences. The organisers of such events are attracted by his status rather than his speaking ability.

However, last night at a business function he started off by asking: 'Can you hear me at the back of the room?'

And a voice from the back shouted: 'Yes. But I'd be pleased to change places with someone who can't.'


**1190.** At the end of his speech he left his audience openmouthed – they all yawned at the same time.


**1191.** A guarantee of freedom of speech is not much use unless there is another guarantee of freedom *after* the speech.

# SPORTS & GAMES

**1192.** The main difference between a hunter and an angler is that a hunter lies in wait, while an angler waits and lies.

**1193.** Give a man a fish and he will have food for a day. Teach him how to fish and you can get him out of the house every Saturday.

**1194.** My wife recently joined an aerobics class and she gets a lot of exercise. She's never actually managed to get to the class – but she spends a tremendous amount of time and energy trying to put on her leotard.

**1195.** If God had wanted me to touch my toes he would have put them on my thighs.

**1196.** The only exercise he gets is jumping to wrong conclusions.

**1197.** My wife keeps telling me to get in shape. But I told her I *am* in shape – *round* is a shape.

**1198.** In order to advance his career, Sebastian decided to take up golf. After his first morning on the golf course his wife asked him: 'How did it go?'

'Seventy-two strokes!' said Sebastian.

'That's wonderful,' said his wife.

'It took me seventy-two strokes,' said Sebastian, 'just to hit the first ball.'

**1199.** He went to his priest and asked, 'Is it a sin to play golf on Sunday?'

The priest replied, 'I've seen you on the golf course several times. The way you play it's a sin any day.'

**1200.** The police arrested him for killing his wife with a golf club.

'Her injuries show that you hit her with the club nine times,' said one of the policeman.

'Oh,' said the arrested man, 'Couldn't you put it down as a five or six?'

**1201.** Nigel likes to play rugby – even though it's a very rough game. After the match on Saturday he came home with three broken teeth, a torn ear and a broken nose. I wish he would give them back to the players he took them from.

**1202.** His baseball team are known as The Scrambled Eggs – they are always getting beaten.

**1203.** The house was on fire. A woman appeared at an upstairs window. She was clutching a baby and screaming, 'My baby! My baby! Save my baby!'

'Throw the baby down to me!' shouted a young man. 'I'll catch him.'

'You might drop him,' shouted the woman.

'I'm a professional footballer,' shouted the man. 'I'm a goalkeeper. I'm very good at catching. The baby will be safe with me.'

The woman threw down the baby to the young man who put all his professional expertise into operation, and he expertly caught the baby and then, unthinkingly, kicked it over the garden wall.

**1204.** Last weekend I did something I've never done before – I went fly fishing: and caught a three ounce fly!

**1205.** 'Dad, Dad!' said Gareth. 'I think I've been selected for the school football team.'

'That's good,' replied Gareth's father. 'But why do you only *think* you've been selected? Aren't you sure? What position will you play?'

'Well,' said Gareth, 'it's not been announced officially, but I overheard the football coach tell my teacher that if I was in the team I'd be a great draw-back.'

**1206.** My wife and son were watching a football match on TV when my son got excited and shouted, 'Pass the ball! Pass the ball! Why won't the idiot pass the ball to Smith?'

'Well,' said my wife, 'you can't really expect a footballer who cost a million pounds to pass the ball to a player who cost a lot less.'

**1207.** When I was a young boy all the other kids insisted that I was in the football team. They said I was vital to the game. They couldn't possibly play without me. They needed me. After all, I was the only one with a football.

**1208.** Mrs Brown was fed up with her husband being forever out of the house and playing golf.

'Why can't you stay at home a bit more?' she asked.

'Because it's fun on the golf course,' replied her husband. 'And it's good exercise.'

'Maybe I should try it, too?' suggested Mrs Brown.

'You probably wouldn't like it,' said Mr Brown. 'All the walking might tire you out. Why don't you stay at home with your knitting and the TV?'

But Mrs Brown insisted that her husband took her to the golf club and gave her lessons.

The very first day together on the course, her husband's first shot was appalling, but he told his wife, 'There! That's how to hit the ball. Another two or three strokes and that'll be it.'

Mrs Brown then took her first ever shot – and scored a hole in one.

Mr Brown was amazed. He was speechless.

The couple walked over to where the ball nestled in the hole and Mrs Brown said, 'That wasn't very good, was it? It's going to be very difficult to hit the ball out of this little hole.'

**1209.** The reason I don't play polo is because I think it must be incredibly difficult to ride a horse while using a stick to hit little mints.

**1210.** She used to be an all-round sportswoman but as she got older, she just became all-round.

**1211.** I told my wife that we had been invited on a shooting weekend in Scotland.

'Oh good!' she said. 'Now I can see those strange birds that wear trousers.'

'Strange birds that wear trousers?' I asked.

'Yes,' she replied. 'People are always saying they shoot pheasants in braces.'

# THEATRE & THE ACTING WORLD

**1212.** The actress had just moved into the area and was registering her children with the local doctor. 'I've got five children – all boys,' she told the doctor's receptionist.

'First name?' asked the receptionist.

'They're all called George,' replied the woman. The receptionist was surprised. 'Each of them has the first name George?' she asked.

'Yes,' replied the actress.

'But what happens when you call out "George" – how do they know which one you want?'

'That's easy. I've been married five times and they've each got a different surname so I use that.'

**1213.** He's fresh from his success with a one man show – only one man showed up to see it.

**1214.** When the actress was asked why she had candles on her wedding cake, she replied: 'Well, it *is* an annual event.'

**1215.** The Hollywood actress liked her tenth husband so much she decided to keep him for an extra fortnight.

**1216.** The young actress was delighted to get a part with real meat in it. She had to dress up as a bun for a commercial for hamburgers.

**1217.** I was once asked to play the part of a vampire's victim in a Hollywood movie, but I turned it down. I don't do bit parts.

**1218.** The leading actress was most upset on her opening night. She only received seventeen bouquets of flowers. Yet she had paid the florist to send twenty.

**1219.** I've just been to see a hit play – most of the cast were hit by rotten eggs and tomatoes.

**1220.** The last time I was in London I went to a theatre ticket office and the man in front of me in the queue asked the box office clerk, 'Can I have a ticket for tonight's performance?'

'Certainly sir,' replied the clerk. 'Would you like to be in the stalls?'

'No,' said the man. 'I'm not an animal – I want a proper seat.'

**1221.** I've just got a speaking part in the theatre. I have to walk up and down saying, 'Programmes. Would anyone like a programme?'

**1222.** A young lady I know in Hollywood has just arranged her wedding for 7 o'clock in the morning – that way, if the marriage doesn't work out, she will still have most of the morning left.

**1223.** What would Shakespeare be doing if he was alive today?

Shouting and scratching at the lid on his coffin.

# TRANSPORT

**1224.** If your teenage son insists on learning to drive, it is best not to stand in his way.

**1225.** His son came to him and said: 'Dad, I've got some good news and some bad news. You know you kindly let me borrow your car last night? Well, the good news is that the car's air bags work ...'

**1226.** Men never get lost while driving a car – they just investigate a variety of alternative destinations.

**1227.** The driver of a lorry loaded with the latest edition of a thesaurus swerved to avoid a cat and crashed into a tree. The driver was reported as being stunned, shocked, jolted, taken aback by the unexpected, unanticipated, unpredicted, unforeseeable, unannounced, unheralded event, misfortune, bad luck accident.

**1228.** He's just got rid of the terrible knocking noise in his car. He decided to stop travelling with his highly critical wife.

**1229.** When he fell asleep on the plane and suddenly awoke, trembling and panic-stricken from a horrible nightmare, he quickly pressed the call button for the *fright* attendant.

**1230.** The plane suddenly seemed to rock about and the captain turned on the public address system and said: 'There's nothing to worry about. It's just a mechanical problem. The two engines seem to have lost a bit of power and one of them is on fire – so I'm just putting on my parachute and going for help.'

**1231.** The plane went into a steep dive. The pilot announced: 'We have a problem. Stay calm and pray. We're doing all we can to fix things.'

The plane then began to come out of the dive, but then jolted and shuddered, and passengers could see that one of the plane's engines was on fire.

'I can't die like this!' shouted a woman. 'I'm twenty-five and no man has ever made me feel like a *real* woman. I must have a *real* man *now*!'

A young man sitting behind her ripped off his shirt, displaying his rippling muscles and the woman sighed. Her pleas had brought her this gorgeous hunk.

'I can make you feel like a *real* woman,' he said as he handed her his shirt and said, 'Iron this.'

**1232.** The first time I went to Bournemouth I wanted to visit Compton Acres Gardens in Poole. So I joined a bus queue, and as a bus approached I asked the elderly lady in front of me, 'Excuse me, does this bus go to Compton Acres?'

'Yes,' replied the lady, 'just get off the bus two stops before the stop I get off.'

**1233.** The car dealer tried to sell me a car that he said was in mint condition. It had a hole in the middle.

**1234.** I was nearly late arriving at this meeting. The journey from my home was extremely arduous and I had to walk the last few miles after I suddenly lost control of my car – the finance company re-possessed it.

**1235.** I bought a car that was rust free. The car dealer sold me the car for £2,000 and didn't charge anything for all the rust.

**1236.** I know a man whose car is in such bad condition that when he took it to the garage and told a mechanic, 'Give it a service', they gave it a burial service.

**1237.** Frederick: My cousin thinks he's a car.

Julia: What does he do?

Frederick: He makes car-like noises and jogs along the road instead of the pavement. When he gets to a petrol station he pours petrol in the back pocket of his trousers.

Julia: Shouldn't you do something about it?

Frederick: I suppose I should, but I need the money he gives me. Every Saturday he pays me £35 to give him a good wax and polish.

**1238.** What is the difference between an ancient car and a class in school?

Not much – they both have lots of nuts and a crank at the front.


**1239.** When buying an old second-hand car always insist on getting one with heated rear windows. That way, in winter you can warm your hands while you're pushing it.


**1240.** When the professor of mathematics was involved in a car crash, he was asked by a police officer if he could remember the other car's registration number.

'Not exactly,' replied the professor, 'but the total of the numbers divided by the last digit was equal to the square root of the second number.'


**1241.** I was on a walk in Dorset, lost in thought, when a car pulled up beside me and a fat gentleman wound down his car window and shouted, 'Yokel! Do you know the way to Bournemouth?'

'Yes,' I replied, and continued walking.


**1242.** Policeman: Madam, I have just recorded you as 50 at least.

Female speeding motorist: Don't be ridiculous, officer! These clothes always make me look a lot older.


**1243.** I was on a plane the other day, sitting next to an elderly woman who was on her first flight.

Just before take-off, the stewardess came round with some boiled sweets and explained to the elderly woman that the sweets would help to reduce the pressure in her ears.

Half an hour after take-off, the elderly woman asked the stewardess if it was now all right to take the sweets out of her ears.

**1244.** 'Why did you become a driver for the railway?'

'It was the only way I was sure of getting a seat on a train.'

**1245.** I was on a plane from Moscow to New York when a man got up from a seat a few rows behind me and began to walk down the aisle towards the toilets and the front of the plane.

He looked rather menacing. He was wearing scruffy jeans and a bulky leather jacket which was firmly zipped up. His hands were in his jacket pockets.

Suddenly he stopped. He looked to where I was sitting and said, 'Hijack.'

I was terrified. He said the word again, even louder, 'Hijack!'

The man sitting next to me put down the copy of *The Astute Private Investor*, an excellent book which he had been reading. He looked up at the man in the aisle and said, 'Hi George. How are you? I didn't know you were on this plane, too.'

**1246.** As the plane flew over the sea, I saw something large, black and hairy in the water. It was an oil wig.

**1247.** The only reason the railways in Britain print timetables is so passengers know how late their trains have been.

**1248.** The handsome young man was about to set off on a round-the-world yacht trip when his sextant was stolen.

He went into a shop on the quay and asked the new, attractive young female assistant, 'Do you have a sextant?'

'Why do it in a tent?' she asked. 'You can come back to my flat if you like.'

**1249.** Suddenly, out at sea in our small sailing boat, we heard a loud noise, 'Croak, croak' it went. 'Croak, croak.' It was a frog-horn.

**1250.** I knew it was going to be a plane flight with a difference when a naked man rushed down the aisle shouting, 'This is your captain streaking ...'